What people are saying about *The Seven Deadly Sayings of Nonprofit Leaders*...

Reid Zimmerman has identified these seven deadly sayings through years of work with nonprofits of every ilk, and his vignettes ring familiar to anyone who's paid attention to their own organizations. This book is to be used again and again as a guide to make your organization better one step at a time. Don't miss this opportunity. Your organization's sustainability depends on it.

Kristi Rendahl
Organizational Development Advisor, Center for Victims of Torture

The Seven Deadly Sayings *is an effective and jarring wake-up call for nonprofit boards and managers. Nonprofit leaders soon realize that running a nonprofit organization looks easier from the outside than it is. The actual nonprofit experience is a complex set of choices and relationships, and Reid Zimmerman has given us a very useful set of tools to bring these critical challenges to life.*

Jon Pratt
Executive Director, Minnesota Council of Nonprofits

Reid Zimmerman employs his razor-sharp insights and experience in the trenches to bring this book to life. His compelling messages remind us to fear complacency, and his common-sense tools empower us to pursue excellence. I highly recommend Zimmerman's work as a quick and valuable read for busy nonprofit executives and boards, one that can inspire powerful conversations.

Matt Kilian
Vice President for External Relations and *IQ* Magazine Executive Editor, Initiative Foundation

Reid Zimmerman doesn't just validate the importance of nonprofit organizations to the well-being of our people, communities, and nation. He does much, much more. Inside **The Seven Deadly Sayings***, Zimmerman provides a guide on how to efficiently and smoothly operate a nonprofit organization. We owe him a great debt of gratitude for the insight and wisdom he shares. He uses real-life examples from his decades of teaching and consulting to make the seven deadly sayings come alive. This book is a must-read if you are improvement driven.*

Dan Hoffman
Executive Director, Minnesota Agriculture and Rural Leadership Program

Reid Zimmerman is the quintessential reflective practitioner—especially insightful about the theory-practice connection—and his book presents the hard-won wisdom of an in-the-trenches reflective practitioner. **Seven Deadly Sayings** *provides an effective conceptual framework for inquiring deeply into core elements of nonprofit effectiveness and continuous learning. Use it not just to absorb its wisdom, which is substantial, but also use it to deepen your own commitment to and engagement in reflective practice, for reflection on experience is the best teacher.*

Michael Quinn Patton
Former President, American Evaluation Association, and Author of Six Program Evaluation and Research Methods Books

Reid Zimmerman brings years of "pracademics" (practical experience and academic discipline) to the field of nonprofit management. In his **Seven Deadly Sayings***, he uses a common-sense approach and provides a substantive guide to successful nonprofit leadership. The book is also fun to read.*

Jim Scheibel
Former Mayor of Saint Paul, Minnesota, and Nonprofit Executive

With "plain talk," Reid Zimmerman both illuminates the dynamics that hold back nonprofit managers and paints a clear picture of how "to get better." His suggestions are neither scary nor difficult to implement. **Seven Deadly Sayings** *is an easy-read operations manual that should be required reading for all staff and board members.*

Eve Borenstein
Nonprofit Attorney, Borenstein and McVeigh Law Office LLC

The
Seven Deadly Sayings
of Nonprofit Leaders

...And How to Avoid Them

Reid A. Zimmerman, PhD, CFRE

PRESS

The Seven Deadly Sayings of Nonprofit Leaders…And How to Avoid Them

One of the **In the Trenches**™ series

Published by
CharityChannel Press, an imprint of CharityChannel LLC
30021 Tomas, Suite 300
Rancho Santa Margarita, CA 92688-2128 USA

CharityChannel.com

Copyright © 2014 Read A. Zimmerman

All rights reserved. No part of this book shall be reproduced, stored in a retrieval system, or transmitted by any means, electronic, mechanical, photocopying, recording, or otherwise, without written permission from the publisher. No patent liability is assumed with respect to the use of the information contained herein. This publication contains the opinions and ideas of its author. It is intended to provide helpful and informative material on the subject matter covered. It is sold with the understanding that the author and publisher are not engaged in rendering professional services in the book. If the reader requires personal assistance or advice, a competent professional should be consulted. The author and publisher specifically disclaim any responsibility for any liability, loss, or risk, personal or otherwise, that is incurred as a consequence, directly or indirectly, of the use and application of any of the contents of this book. Although every precaution has been taken in the preparation of this book, the publisher and author assume no responsibility for errors or omissions. No liability is assumed for damages resulting from the use of information contained herein.

In the Trenches, In the Trenches logo, and book design are trademarks of CharityChannel Press, an imprint of CharityChannel LLC.

ISBN Print Book: 978-1-9380775-1-7 | ISBN eBook: 978-1-9380775-2-4

Library of Congress Control Number: 2014934641

13 12 11 10 9 8 7 6 5 4 3 2 1

Printed in the United States of America

This and most CharityChannel Press books are available at special quantity discounts for bulk purchases for sales promotions, premiums, fundraising, or educational use. For information, contact CharityChannel Press, 30021 Tomas, Suite 300, Rancho Santa Margarita, CA 92688-2128 USA. +1 949-589-5938

Publisher's Acknowledgments

This book was produced by a team dedicated to excellence; please send your feedback to editors@charitychannel.com.

We first wish to acknowledge the tens of thousands of peers who call charitychannel.com their online professional home. Your enthusiastic support for the **In the Trenches**™ series is the wind in our sails.

Members of the team who produced this book include:

Editors

Acquisitions Editor: Linda Lysakowski

Comprehensive Editor: Susan Schaefer

Copy Editor: Jill McLain

Production

In the Trenches Series Design: Deborah Perdue

Layout Editor: Jill McLain

Administrative

CharityChannel LLC: Stephen Nill, CEO

Marketing and Public Relations: John Millen and Linda Lysakowski

About the Author

Dr. Reid A. Zimmerman has over thirty years' experience in the social sector, having served as an executive director, vice president of development, communications director, and board member for a number of organizations in Minnesota. A Certified Fund Raising Executive (CFRE), Reid has extensive experience in fundraising, organizational development, strategic planning, program evaluation, and performance management.

He is the Honorary Professor of Practice at Hamline University in St. Paul, Minnesota, teaching nonprofit and public administration management and leadership. Additionally he is an adjunct professor of nonprofit management at Capella and St. Thomas Universities.

Reid works and volunteers across the United States and Canada as a respected and highly rated trainer, seminar leader, speaker, and facilitator. He is an evaluator for the Performance Excellence Network, member of the development committee for the Minnesota Council of Nonprofits *Principles and Practices of Nonprofit Excellence* (1994, 2005, and 2013), and author of articles on nonprofit leadership, fundraising, and evaluation. Reid's teaching as well as his planning, evaluation, and fundraising consulting work provide him contact with hundreds of nonprofit leaders and practitioners each year.

Reid holds undergraduate degrees in sociology/psychology and secondary education, a master of divinity, and a PhD in organizational development, change, and effectiveness, focusing on nonprofit performance.

He lives in rural Minnesota with his wife, Lori, and daughters. You can reach him at reidazimmerman@gmail.com.

Dedication

To all of my favorite women—my wife, Lori, and daughters, Darthy, Lissa, Ali, Megan, and Hannah—who remind me every day what it is to love and be loved. Thank you.

Author's Acknowledgments

It is often challenging to differentiate between a mentor, colleague, friend, and/or peer. Many of the people to whom I owe credit for ideas and content of this brief manuscript blur the lines of those characterizations.

I need to thank many associates at the Minnesota Council of Nonprofits, especially Jon Pratt, the executive director, several of his staff, and past members of the board of directors, Jim Toscano and Dr. Michael Wirth-Davis who, along with Kate Barr, Dr. Cathy Gustafson, and Jim Scheibel, are also cofaculty at Hamline University.

Brian Lassiter, the president and CEO of the Performance Excellence Network, has been instrumental in firmly grounding me in the National Baldrige Excellence Program and introduced me to Dr. Mark Blazey, quality trainer extraordinaire.

Dr. Michael Q. Patton, my mentor and dissertation advisor, helped me formulate and synthesize many of the ideas that have found a home in this book.

My students also challenge me, and I need to acknowledge that. I have been privileged to dialogue and work with some excellent young nonprofit leaders who regularly debate nonprofit leadership ideas and concepts with me. Some report back very quickly on the impact they see from executing ideas and practices we have discussed in graduate seminars or discovered in their own research. For that dialogue and input, I am always grateful.

I also want to recognize you, the nonprofit leader who is reading this book. I ask that you help keep this dialogue open and vibrant. It is only as we work to help each other become better that we, as major influencers of that which is good in our world, will become effective enough to be called the *first* sector of our society rather than the third.

> *He that knew all that learning ever writ*
> *Knew only this—that he knew nothing yet.*
>
> –Aphra Behn (1640-1689)

Contents

Foreword xvii

Introduction xix

Chapter One
The Seven Sayings: Do You Hear What I Hear? 1

Chapter Two
The Basics of Accomplishment and Assessment 7

Chapter Three
Mission, Vision, and Values—Without Which There Are No Questions 13

Chapter Four
Deadly Saying One: "Who's In Charge around Here Anyway?" 23

Chapter Five
Deadly Saying Two: "Somehow We'll Get By... We Usually Do!" 39

Chapter Six
Deadly Saying Three: "We Know What's Best for Our Clients" 51

Chapter Seven
Deadly Saying Four, "My Intuition Is Usually Right" 61

Chapter Eight
Deadly Saying Five: "Our Staff and Volunteers Are Simply the Best!" 71

Chapter Nine
Deadly Saying Six: "We've Never Done It That Way Before" 81

Chapter Ten
Deadly Saying Seven: "We're Doing Pretty Well This Year" 93

Chapter Eleven
In the Beginning, or Once Upon a Time..103

Chapter Twelve
Leading a Healthy Organization..109

Appendix A
Principles and Practices of Nonprofit Excellence 115

Appendix B
Samples of National and State Standards of Excellence.......................117

Appendix C
Template for Strategic and Operational Planning 119

Index..121

Summary of Chapters

Chapter One
The Seven Sayings: Do You Hear What I Hear? These are seven sayings that can lead to the death of a nonprofit organization—unless, of course, someone takes action when they are spoken, whispered, or suggested. What are they?

Chapter Two
The Basics of Accomplishment and Assessment. These documents and ideas form the basis and methodology for assessing the principles of nonprofit effectiveness and excellence. Consider what other documents or tools your organization might use to determine how it is doing or where you can find recommendations for improvement.

Chapter Three
Mission, Vision, and Values—Without Which There Are No Questions. A nonprofit provides little value for the community without clearly articulating who it is, what it does, what it sees as a bright future, and what values it espouses. Does your organization capture these issues in its mission, vision, and values?

Chapter Four
Deadly Saying One: "Who's In Charge around Here Anyway?" No issue is more critical to a nonprofit than its leadership. There are several kinds of leadership, each as important as the other in its respective position and relationships. What is the quality of your organization's leadership?

Chapter Five
Deadly Saying Two: "Somehow We'll Get By... We Usually Do!" Planning, budgets, measurement, goals, and activities are all critical components and useful means for doing good and not just doing. Are you using these powerful tools to help you be the best you can possibly be?

Chapter Six
Deadly Saying Three: "We Know What's Best for Our Clients." Customers or clients need to feel like they are respected and that the services they receive are valuable to them. Do you know how your clients feel about your organization or its services and programs? Do you know what motivates and satisfies them?

Chapter Seven
Deadly Saying Four: "My Intuition Is Usually Right." Gathering data and understanding them is critical to effective performance of an organization. What information do you have and use to provide effective and efficient services to your clients?

Chapter Eight
Deadly Saying Five: "Our Staff and Volunteers Are Simply the Best!" I expect that they are. But how do you steward this human resource? Do you understand their needs? How do you treat them, really?

Chapter Nine
Deadly Saying Six: "We've Never Done It That Way Before." Knowing how a service gets provided or an activity gets completed is critical to making it better. Do you really understand how the processes of your organization or programs work?

Chapter Ten
Deadly Saying Seven: "We're Doing Pretty Well This Year." Demonstrating effectiveness requires that you have measures to support your claims. Counting numbers of program participants or hours of service provided does not mean you are doing a good job at changing or improving people's lives. Do you have the evidence to prove your organization performs well and creates a positive impact in your community?

Chapter Eleven
In the Beginning, or Once Upon a Time… I share some of the principles, practices, and professional associations that helped me through my early years leading nonprofit organizations.

Chapter Twelve
Leading a Healthy Organization. Here are ten suggestions and a few additional ideas for using the concepts in this book, leading, and moving your organization to be the best it can be for your clients and the community.

Foreword

The need to improve your nonprofit's performance has perhaps never been greater. The challenging economy over the last few years has intensified the need for thoughtful improvement and meaningful change within *all* nonprofits. Stakeholders—clients, patients, residents, patrons, members, constituents, customers—expect more, competent workers are growing scarce, the demand for volunteers' time is increasing, and competition for funding is intensifying. All at a time when the demand for programs and services is steadily growing. But—with the complexity of today's nonprofits—where does one start? How do you know on which areas of your agency's operations to focus?

In *The Seven Deadly Sayings*, Reid captures the essence of continuous improvement for today's nonprofits. He clearly articulates why nonprofit leaders need to improve their agencies (to grow and sustain their nonprofit missions), the importance of diagnosing current agency performance (through assessment), where to focus your improvement efforts (on the seven key areas represented by the deadly sayings), and how to close the gap (providing ideas for improvement, best practices, and helpful hints).

I have known Reid for over a decade, and I can attest to his deep nonprofit acumen and his keen insights on what it takes to improve organizational performance. (But you don't need to take my word on it—just read for yourself!) In *The Seven Deadly Sayings*, his use of stories and case studies to convey nonprofit truisms is masterful. The scenarios he offers certainly resonate with me, as I'm sure they do with most nonprofit executives—they encourage reflection on what's truly important to nonprofits' success and provide real examples regarding the challenges nonprofits face. He also offers a useful compendium of "Blue Ribbon" and "Gold Cup" best practices in practical formats, including checklists and red, yellow, and green as stoplight indicators.

The foundation of Reid's insights is the *Criteria for Performance Excellence* of the Baldrige framework, which represent the leading edge of validated management practice—a set of best practices have been *proven* to drive and sustain superior outcomes in nonprofits and businesses alike. Reid is an expert in this framework, and he has seen those principles—along with the Principles and Practices of Nonprofit Excellence and the Charities Review Council accountability standards—applied to dozens of successful (and not-so-successful) nonprofits. But what makes this book so handy is its practicality: Reid has taken complex concepts and positioned them in an easy-to-read, easy-to-implement format.

In fact, it has been said that the Baldrige framework is too complex, which is the reason many nonprofit leaders give for not using it to optimize their organizations' resources and improve their outcomes. But Reid has translated it into a helpful set of guidelines that could be summarized in three simple—yet powerful—questions:

1. Is your nonprofit any good?

2. Is it getting better?

3. How do you know?

If you can answer those three questions definitively, your agency will be well on the way to achieving higher performance and sustaining superior outcomes. And Reid's book will guide you through the key areas—leadership, planning, customer focus, measurement, workforce focus, and process—that define nonprofit "goodness."

I would recommend you read the book cover to cover, taking notes (as I did), and completing the checklists and assessments. And then do it again. Share it with your board and your key stakeholders. Use it in the way in which it was intended—as a user's guide to help your organization improve.

Improving nonprofit performance in today's environment is tough, but that's not a good excuse for not trying. Vince Lombardi once said: "Perfection is not possible. But if we chase perfection, we might just reach excellence." Best wishes on your journey to excellence.

Brian Lassiter, CEO
Performance Excellence Network

Introduction

In 1980, fresh from graduate school, I was hired as the associate director of a relatively large nonprofit organization. There were over three thousand members, a substantial facility, a seven-figure budget, and a staff of more than twenty-five. A month after I was hired, the founding executive director of thirty years resigned and retired because of a disagreement with the board of directors. The responsibility for managing this organization fell to me.

I did not have a clue about management. My undergraduate and graduate work had been almost all liberal arts and programmatically oriented. I had a total of three elective credits in "management" under my belt. Woefully unprepared and feeling more than inadequate, I did what I could, seeking help from the board of directors, another program director, and a formally retired part-time staff member who provided practical advice based on the wisdom of his years.

While this nonprofit organization happened to be a large suburban church and parochial school, and the resigning executive director was the senior and founding pastor, the situation is quite similar to that encountered by many nonprofit leaders, perhaps by you.

Educated as social workers, artists, nurses, and teachers, or with a myriad of other professional skills, we find ourselves having leadership, management, and accountability for the operation of a nonprofit organization thrust upon us. Few nonprofit leaders of the past several decades have come into the profession prepared with a degree in business or nonprofit management.

> Educated as social workers, artists, nurses, teachers, or with a myriad of other professional skills, we find ourselves having leadership, management, and accountability for the operation of a nonprofit organization thrust upon us.
>
> **observation**

In my case, I had a bachelor of arts in liberal arts and theology and a bachelor of science in secondary education. My 125-credit master of divinity degree was strong on exegesis, homiletics, hermeneutics, apologetics, and ancient languages—and very short on parish administration. The three elective credits mentioned earlier hardly prepared me to develop a budget, direct staff, manage the facility, plan for the future, or do fundraising. Yet all of those things were immediately required of me.

Six months later, a new senior pastor arrived and relieved me of much of that responsibility. He, however, had not received any formal management training either. He simply had more experience, more opportunity for trial and error, and was smart enough to learn from earlier mistakes.

My Resolve

Based on the trauma and tension of that experience, I resolved to learn more. And so I sought seminars and courses in parish administration. A few years later, as an executive director of a small human services organization, I enrolled in the same kinds of courses for nonprofit administration. Later still, I discovered additional information about nonprofit leadership and effectiveness during my doctoral studies in organizational development. And, I gained experience along the way as an executive director, grantwriter, administrator, interim executive director, development officer, communications and marketing director, board member, consultant, and educator.

The wise and philosophical author of the biblical book of Ecclesiastes purports in the first chapter that "what has been will be again, what has been done will be done again; there is nothing new under the sun." So it is with the ideas in this book. While I have been witness and privy to the stories, problems, examples, issues, benefits, positives, and negatives described herein, the ideas are not completely my own. They find their roots in the collective minds of people more intelligent and experienced than am I.

The concepts of this book are compiled and coalesced from experts, academic sources, and best practices, and then they are filtered through thirty years of leading, managing, teaching, and consulting with nonprofit organizations. I share these events and resources with you in the hope that you may benefit from them as well.

I've been witness to all of these seven deadly sayings at one time or another in those three decades. Several of them I've heard quite frequently. Funders have shared some of them; others have been uttered by members of my boards of directors and those of other organizations. Executive directors and program managers have stated others, either overheard or with me directly. My students have discussed hearing them as part of their fieldwork experiences. Colleagues on faculty or in the sector tell me they hear them as well. I know you have too.

> The deadliness of these sayings lies in the fact that they point to more serious problems in an organization.
>
> **observation**

"But why do you call them deadly, Zimmerman? I've not known of many nonprofit organizations to fall apart simply because someone made an off-the-cuff remark. How are they deadly?"

Their deadliness lies in the fact that they point to more serious problems in an organization. A sneeze, cough, and red, puffy eyes can point to either a menacing allergy or a deadly influenza. In much the same way, the sayings can either be troublesome and get in the way of providing better service to your clients or indicate the presence of a debilitating flaw in the organizational structure. Either way, the sayings indicate that something is not quite right and needs either self-treatment or a visit to the doctor.

These sayings will continue to be expressed as long as new organizations are formed, new leaders rise up, and boards of directors change membership. As long as people are not perfect and they struggle in imperfect organizations, these sayings, or similar permutations, will be with us.

But they do not need to be deadly sayings. There are leadership practices and management tactics that can prevent them from being uttered or, if spoken, can lessen the negative impact on your organization.

Not Just Stories, Anecdotes, and Vignettes

At the beginning of each chapter, you will find several stories. Stories convey the essence of this book. Listen to them… Learn from them. Stories, after all, are the most effective conveyors of information—and often truth.

These stories are not fictitious. They all have a place in reality. Some of them are personal experiences and are indicated as such by the use of the personal pronoun. They are recaptured as accurately as my memory will allow and relayed with as little bias as possible.

> If you find some of the stories and anecdotes a bit humorous or even comical, it means you understand the message they convey. I hope you do.
>
> **food for thought**

Other vignettes have been developed based on situations I have witnessed, stories shared with me, or conversations I've overhead in my years of working and consulting with nonprofit leaders and organizations.

While the names of real people and organizations have been changed to protect both the innocent and the guilty, you might find yourself thinking you know people or organizations described in the stories. And probably you do, because they are common situations.

These anecdotes or stories are not meant to illuminate the point of the chapter. They *are* the point! The stories are as important as the questions and other aspects of the rest of the book.

I hope you find yourself, your organization, your staff, and your friends in these stories and learn from them. If you chuckle at some of them, it means you understand. I hope you do.

Chapter One

The Seven Sayings: Do You Hear What I Hear?

IN THIS CHAPTER

- What are the seven deadly sayings?
- Why the sayings can be deadly
- Seven deadly sayings for whom?

Somewhat like the seven deadly sins, the seven deadly sayings are often buried beneath and interwoven in the very nature of our social-sector organizations. While there may be other "deadly" sayings, and the phrasing may differ from situation to situation, many of the challenges faced by organizations in our sector can be encapsulated by snippets of their leaders' conversations, attitudes, or behaviors.

The sayings are spoken by executive directors and program managers, by board chairs and volunteers, by line staff, and sometimes even by donors. The sayings are said with varying degrees of challenge, sarcasm, questioning, naiveté, or emotion. They are "deadly" sayings because when they are spoken or implied, something is wrong; something is potentially deadly for the organization.

Deadly Saying One: "Who's In Charge around Here Anyway?"

This first question is about leadership. The reason it is first is that there is no issue more critical to a nonprofit. There are several kinds of leadership, each as important as the other in its respective position and relationships. What is the quality of your organization's leadership?

Deadly Saying Two: "Somehow We'll Get By... We Usually Do!"

Planning, budgets, measurement, goals, and activities are all critical components of doing good (making positive change) and not just doing. Are you using these powerful tools to help you be the best you can possibly be, or are you just "getting by"?

Deadly Saying Three: "We Know What's Best for Our Clients"

Customers or clients need to feel valued and believe that the services they receive are valuable to them. Do you know how your clients feel about your organization or its services and programs? Have you asked them? Do you really know what they want and need?

> These are "deadly" sayings because when they are spoken or implied, something is wrong; something is potentially deadly for the organization.
>
> **observation**

Deadly Saying Four: "My Intuition Is Usually Right"

Gathering data and understanding them is critical to effectively managing the performance of an organization. What information do you have and use to provide effective and efficient services to your clients?

Deadly Saying Five: "Our Staff and Volunteers Are Simply the Best!"

I expect that they are. But do you understand their needs? How do you treat them, really? Are you valuing, rewarding, and stewarding the human resources of your organization in the most beneficial manner?

Deadly Saying Six: "We've Never Done It That Way Before"

Knowing and really understanding the process by which a service gets provided or an activity gets completed is critical to making it better. Do you really understand how the systems and processes of your organization or programs work?

Deadly Saying Seven: "We're Doing Pretty Well This Year"

Demonstrating effectiveness requires that you have outcome measures to support your claims. Counting numbers of program participants or hours of service provided does not mean you are doing a good job. Do you have the evidence to prove your organization has actually changed lives? Is your organization really performing well? How do you know?

The sayings we have just considered and some of the challenging questions they present are the beginning of this work. Your approach to investigating their significance for your organization will make a big difference in the ability of your organization to achieve effectiveness and excellence.

And, as we will see later, the challenge of leadership is to confront the deadliness of these questions in an unflinching manner, deal with them, and develop a means to answer them. I hope you will read on and do just that.

Why the Sayings Can Be Deadly

These expressions of frustration or questioning, innocence, or perhaps even hostility often reveal more about what is going on in a situation than the remarks suggest. There is sometimes fear captured in these sayings. Fear that we feel circumstantially trapped or that we do not have the skill and knowledge to change things. Sometimes the comments get directed at individuals when we really need to change the process or the system to improve the situation. Sometimes, though, we despair and blame the situation or circumstances when, in reality, the people involved need training or support to be better leaders or managers.

> The seven sayings are deadly only if they are repeated, not challenged, and enclose our minds and beings.
>
> **food for thought**

There is sometimes an air of arrogance among nonprofit leaders who believe we have all, or at least most of, the answers. Our training as educators, health care providers, social workers, counselors, and practitioners encourages us to share our knowledge with others, and we are often more than willing to tell our clients what they need to do to improve their situation. This attitude causes us to continue to search inside ourselves for answers that are not there. Asking for outside help is often antithetical to our training. These sayings are certainly deadly when they contain and continue this arrogant attitude.

Sometimes these sayings indicate that serious things are wrong. New legislation gets enacted and your organization misses a deadline, causing the forfeit of its 501(c)(3) status. Internal leadership attacks each other rather than the problem. The lack of a financial process demands an unexpected audit that makes the local news and causes donors to pull out. A missing human resource policy results in the organization ending up in a lawsuit that costs thousands of dollars to settle. These are the concerns that cause nonprofit leaders to lose sleep at night.

However, the utterance of one, or even several, of the deadly seven may not indicate a devastating consequence. The situation may not yet have risen to the level requiring CPR or emergency surgery. It may simply be the persistent cough of a process that is not working and needs fixing. These issues do, however, speak to the old adage… for want of a nail, the shoe was lost… for want of the shoe, the horse was lost, and on through the rider, the battle, and the war.

Little issues overlooked or ignored over time can be deadly. It is just that the death or debilitation takes longer. For example, slightly misusing small amounts of designated funding on a regular basis will ultimately have about the same result as embezzlement. The latter is just much more public and more rapid in its destruction of the organization.

Your organization might be working quite well. So why, you may ask, look at the negative? Perhaps we should concentrate on the good things our organizations are accomplishing?

> **watch out!**
> Slightly misusing small amounts of designated funding on a regular basis will ultimately have about the same result as embezzlement.

We should! There are many good things happening in each and every organization working in the social sector. But very isolated indeed is the organization that is like Mary Poppins: "Practically perfect in every way."

We seldom see the doctor when we are feeling perfectly well. And even at our annual physical when everything is pretty good, there is still that gnawing feeling, often validated by our physician, that something could be improved. Our weight, blood pressure, cholesterol, exercise regime (or lack thereof), or diet may be less than great. So, the negatives point out the need for improvement. The things that are working sweetly sometimes mask the deadly flaws in our infrastructure. It is somewhat like the Interstate 35 bridge in Minneapolis that collapsed in August 2007. It was doing a great job of carrying people and vehicles across the Mississippi River... right up until it didn't. Perhaps, through regular investigation, had the internal structure been previously scrutinized, there would not have been such a terrible loss of life and property.

Seven Deadly Sayings for Whom?

This is not a book about you or me. This book is about our organizations. Those living, breathing, real, cuddly and vicious, supercilious and sacrosanct, dirty and truthful organizations filled with human beings who sometimes, but not always, work well together and effectively.

>
> Throughout this book, the term "organization" refers to a formal, legally incorporated, usually 501(c)(3) entity that is governed by a board of directors and, in most cases, has staff members and volunteers.

Sometimes those people and organizations don't function well. And then we need to discover what it is that is wrong. Most of the time it is *not* the human beings that go awry. Most of the time the humans are working hard. Most of the time there is a problem with the *way* things are supposed to work... and don't. And most of the time it is the human beings that get blamed because the *way* is broken.

Most of the work we do is a process. We have a design process or an intake process. There is a fundraising process and a reporting process. Each of these processes is designed to work to produce a result. The questions in this book often ask about your processes. Are they working? Are they working well? Are they working as efficiently as they possibly can? If not, what will it take to make them work better?

Though the Seven Deadly Sayings may seem ominous and fatalistic, the intent of this book is to bring hope that the attitudes expressed in the seven sayings will be the impetus for effective change and positive improvement. Unless the IRS pulls your 501(c)(3) status, as it did to more than three hundred thousand nonprofits in 2011, there is always hope for improvement. We in the nonprofit sector are optimistic souls. We look for what can be and roll up our sleeves to make the world better. The seven sayings are deadly only if they are repeated, not challenged, and enclose our minds and beings.

In the next chapter, we will investigate the approach I suggest as a way of looking at our social sector organizations and how we work. The process of inquiry along with your thoughtful assessment will lead you to more fully understand your own leadership and the practices of your organization.

Future chapters will look more specifically at your mission and seven important areas of organizational effectiveness. Proposed opportunities for improvement and the placement of resources that will have the greatest impact on your organization will be suggested. Ultimately, the purpose is to benefit your clients and your community.

To Recap

- In order to benefit from this book, you need to acknowledge that some of these sayings are being spoken in your organization.

- There are hard questions and lots of work ahead to drive your organization to excellence.

- Are you truly willing, as a nonprofit leader, to take on the challenge of actually addressing the deadly sayings and working to avoid them in your organization?

Chapter Two

The Basics of Accomplishment and Assessment

IN THIS CHAPTER

- Honesty is the best practice
- Leadership for progress, not perfection
- Analyzing your relative position
- Colors and symbols of accomplishment and assessment
- Achievement comes in small steps, not leaps, or: leading the work of assessment

Perhaps the reason you have picked up this book is that you have some interest in helping your nonprofit organization function better, more effectively, or more efficiently.

And why would you want to push your organization in the first place? Because you care! I do anyway, and I hope you do too. I care about the people that our sector educates, heals, houses, feeds, clothes, entertains, speaks on behalf of, cries out for, and cares about. And if we care about these people and causes, we need to care about the organisms, the living, breathing entities called nonprofit organizations that are the vehicle for that care.

Lofty ideals are easy. Understanding your program theory of change is a good start. Putting the ideals and theory into practice and demonstrating results is challenging. Yet we seek and need practical results. If we are going to do any good for our clients, customers, patrons, students, patients, or participants, then we need to see results. We need to see and measure positive changes in their lives, their families, and their position in life and in the community. Ultimately, we want to see positive impact in the community for ourselves, our neighbors, and our children. These are the clients and stakeholders of our nonprofit, the people we ultimately represent and serve.

> The term "stakeholder" designates a person who has an interest in the work you do but who may not be a direct service recipient. That person may be a donor, volunteer, community member, contractor, bureaucrat, or politician. Each does, however, have some investment in your organization.
>
>

Honesty Is the Best Practice

This book is also about truth telling. It will be of no value to you if you attempt to make the situation in your organization appear better than it actually is. Being brutally honest with yourself and the other members of your organization is the only way to get better. It will also be helpful if several people from the same organization answer the questions posed throughout this book. Doing so will provide additional verification of the place where the organization is currently situated. Be tough on yourself. The easy path with the least resistance is not always the one that gets to a positive outcome.

This book is also a guide to performance improvement. In order to improve, you need to know where you are along the continuum of "just making it" to a "world-class performer." Only after you have determined your relative position can you ascertain the next best steps to move your organization forward and upward.

Leadership for Progress, Not Perfection!

This is a book about improvement and progress, not perfection! It is frustrating to feel: "Oh, my gosh!!! Look at all the things we are not doing and need to do!" It is more beneficial to say: "I see where we can make some immediate improvement. Let's try these couple of things and work on them in the next quarter. Then we can see where to go after that."

The challenge of leadership is in determining the most important goals and activities that will accomplish real and measurable improvement. Choose those important few very carefully out of all the potential opportunities that may not have such an immediate impact. This book is about honest evaluation and making informed decisions. It is about getting better over time, not attempting to rush to some idealistic position or stature that will inevitably lead to frustration.

The challenge of leadership for the work of this book is also about setting expectations for the people in your organization. If any positive action is to be taken, any direction attained, any movement begun, it will be so as a result of a leader making it happen. Consider the leadership you provide in your organization and endeavor to work in that sphere of influence to expect, direct, and move that entity forward. Even individuals, managing only themselves, can use the concepts illuminated here to improve the value they provide to clients. A program manager or executive director can have significant impact when really leading the process of discovery and action.

If you are reading this book as someone with a relationship to an organization that is not yet legally incorporated or in receipt of your nonprofit tax status, many of the statements are things to be considered as your organization is formed and begins to function as a legal entity.

Analyzing Your Relative Position

This document is a workbook. That means you will need to get your hands dirty, get down in the muck, and look at the underbelly of the organization with which you affiliate for some portion of every day or week or month. The intensity of that affiliation, the passion that fuels your soul and spirit, and its responsibility for your ability to clothe, house, and feed yourself and your family, will determine how much work you are willing to expend on that organization.

> Finding the most value from this book will be in considering the next most important things you need to do in order for your organization to get better. It is not about accomplishing perfection by next month. It is about taking small steps and progressing to a more solid footing.
>
>

You will be asked throughout the workbook to determine the things you do, the processes you have in place, and the policies extant in your organization. The symbols below will help determine your relative position and suggest where there is work to do. This is where being truthful is critical to allowing the workbook to work for you.

The Colors and Symbols of Accomplishment and Assessment

I often understand things more clearly when presented with a picture, symbol, or story than I do with simply text or script. Symbols carry significant meaning in our lives and often play a vital role in keeping society safe and guiding us to do good work. So, I've chosen symbols to draw our attention to the potential for improvement and as guides for our work.

> Stop on red, slow or approach cautiously on yellow, and go on green. The coloring and meaning are almost universal.
>
>

Stoplights.

We all know their meaning. Stop on red, slow or approach cautiously on yellow, and go on green. The coloring and symbolism are almost universal.

Red–Stop

Red means exactly that. Stop! It means that something is amiss, wrong, or very inappropriate. Legal requirements, governmental regulations, and financial management are the stuff of the Red-Stop level. These must be in place. If your organization discovers errors and omissions in this level, you need to stop and fix them before proceeding. Even if there are many practices in Blue Ribbon or even Gold Cup, a problem in Red-Stop requires immediate attention.

Yellow–Caution

Yellow is the color of ethical practices and transparent behaviors. It considers that, while perhaps not illegal, some of the issues of Yellow-Caution may easily and quickly call a halt to the work of an organization. They are the practices and procedures that make donors think twice about making a donation or an auditor from giving an unqualified opinion. They are also, along with the legalities of Red-Stop, the standards lauded by watchdog organizations as appropriate for the public to consider when supporting an organization.

> Traffic signs and lights are the law of the land: red, yellow, and green. We know what they mean and the consequences of ignoring their direction and warnings. The first three levels are the stop, caution, and go of our nonprofit organizational highways. Pay attention!
>
> **observation**

Green–Go

Green is good! Green is the color of go, growing, and positive action. Green-Go is the arena of meeting the behavioral standards of positive practice. As Kermit the Frog bemoans: "It's not easy being green." He is right! Green-Go involves hard work. Accomplishing the standards of acceptable practice and positive position in the sector takes energy and dedication. But meeting basic standards of accountability is not the ultimate. There is much beyond; more growth and improvement is possible.

Blue Ribbon

A Blue Ribbon demonstrates superior achievement. Becoming a Blue Ribbon organization requires much hard work. Being Blue Ribbon means thoughtful improvement and the attainment of stretch goals. It means teamwork and dedication to meaningful outcomes and community impact.

Gold Cup

When everything is said and done and all the Blue Ribbons have been awarded, judges award the best in show… the Gold Cup. A Gold Cup

> When everything is said and done and all the Blue Ribbons have been awarded, judges award the best of show… the Gold Cup, a trophy for excellence.
>
> **observation**

means preeminent practice. Very few Gold Cups are presented to pies or projects, animals or artwork, or dairy cows or demonstrations at the fair. That is because very few rise to that best-in-class level of quality and expertise.

To get a Gold Cup, your nonprofit organization will need to demonstrate that its practices and procedures, its accomplishments and results, its policies and people are functioning at the highest level of any organization in our society, much less our sector. Excellence in organizational practice and constantly striving at all levels to get better; these are the things of Gold Cups. Attainment of this level of preeminent performance will not happen overnight. Frequently, but not always, it will be mature and confident organizations that rise to this level. I discuss Gold Cup qualities in this workbook to help you realize the benefits of constantly striving for excellence.

As mentioned earlier, honesty is the best policy in interpreting the level of your performance. Don't get hung up on the gradients. Use the symbol levels to begin an honest discussion about making improvement. It is less important to debate your current level of performance than the intent to strive for improvement of practices and procedures that will bring you to the next level.

Achievement Comes in Small Steps, Not Leaps

My wife reminds me regularly when challenged by my teenaged daughters, "Choose your battles." Meaning: Make certain if you are going to fight a good and hard fight that it is a battle you will win and that you will be able to keep control of the territory you have just conquered.

The same thing is true for your work as a nonprofit leader. Choose carefully the steps you want to take on your road to excellence. This workbook is a simple assessment tool. Used appropriately, it can aid you in choosing the battles you need to win as a leader for the benefit of your organization. Some of those battles will be hard.

The CEO of a large multistate nonprofit once told me about her early days in the organization:

"There was only the capacity to look at the bottom line, and I was quickly concerned about this because I realized I was accountable for overall outcomes. I had no idea how to impact the system, because I couldn't understand the health of the system, because I couldn't see into it. I could only see the external balance sheet, and that wasn't enough. So I was very worried about my own accountability to deliver promises to the board of a healthy organization when no one in the organization could even explain to me whether we were healthy or not."

She went on to share with me how difficult it was at times to get her staff and board to understand the importance of clarity of processes and measures in the organization that would ultimately help improve the organization. "Well," she lamented, "it turned out it was really hard because no one wanted to do it." That might be the situation you confront as well, but do not get discouraged. This executive continues to lead and help her organization grow, expand, and provide excellent and needed services.

You will notice that some recommendations appear in an almost duplicative fashion in different contexts though the book. The reason this happens is a result of looking at a similar action or practice from a different view point. Partly it also demonstrates the importance of that practice or activity in the journey of striving for excellence.

Please note as well that when used inappropriately, this assessment tool can cause you to seek changes and actions that will offer only misdirection and potentially cause greater problems for your organization. Understanding the holistic nature of an organization, the systemic manner in which it operates, and the impact of one action on other components of an organism will help you use what you learn here to advance the efficiency and impact of your organization for the greater and collective good.

> Energetically debating your organization's category will not be beneficial. Using the descriptions contained in those levels to improve the ability of your organization to perform is a more useful expenditure of that same energy.
>
> 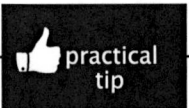 practical tip

Discussion with your whole governance and leadership team will be your best monitor for action. Strive for small advances, simple process improvements, minor accomplishments of quality and satisfaction. Do not attempt to devour the *whole elephant* in one sitting. Fill your plate with a serving you can eat and enjoy.

Do not, however, take anything you read in this book to be perfectly legally accurate and up to date. I am not an attorney and do not espouse to provide legal opinion to you on the basis of anything I have written. Follow the advice of your own legal counsel if in doubt about anything contained in this book.

The colors and symbols will help you contextualize our organization's relative position on a continuum of legal compliance to excellence. Paying attention to those symbols will help you establish your current situation and make positive improvements.

To Recap

- ◆ The benefit of this book is as a workbook. It needs to be used.

- ◆ Honesty is the best policy for using this book. Don't overestimate or inflate your organization's accomplishments or position.

- ◆ It takes real leadership to make improvement. Be that leader and make it happen.

- ◆ It is important to work methodically with the ideas in the book and not attempt them all at once. Aim for small improvements in your processes.

Chapter Three

Mission, Vision, and Values—Without Which There Are No Questions

IN THIS CHAPTER

- Voluntarily supporting a mission
- The vision... your view of the ideal
- To what values do you hold?
- Questions about your mission, vision, and values

It would be unwise of me to start asking you to assess the presence of the deadly questions in your organization without first knowing that you have grounded your organization in its reason for existence.

Why is there a social sector in the USA? What purpose does it serve? Who benefits and why?

Why does your organization exist? Why do you do what you do?

You need to be able to ground the work of your organization in a mission and subsequently develop a solid and articulate mission statement before you look at other aspects of leading and managing that organization.

The impetus to share and care for each other as members of a family and community, if not part of our very human moral fiber and spiritual essence, is certainly embedded in our social mores. Concepts of welfare, charity, and philanthropy can be traced back to the beginnings of every identified religious or moral code of conduct. And for much of known history, those same religious entities managed that sharing and caring as well as supporting expression of the arts, education, and other responsibilities for the quality of life found in that culture.

The last century, however, has witnessed the transfer of much of that responsibility to a different segment of society, that segment we call the third, nonprofit, voluntary, or social sector.

The nonprofit sector of the United States has grown in this last century to about 1.5 million organizations. Currently these nonprofit organizations are responsible for approximately 10 percent of our nation's gross domestic product and a similar percentage of its workforce. They constitute the huge and nationally recognizable as well as the newly incorporated, totally volunteer, single-program, almost-invisible organizations. Nonprofits are both mega health complexes and after-school programs. They are national and international disaster relief agencies and local animal shelters. Universities and theaters, AIDS and ALS support groups, indigenous and immigrant people's organizations, nonprofits are found in every state, region, county, and community in our nation.

In addition, thousands more operate as nongovernmental organizations, with charters in both the United States and many nations around the world. They support the values and qualities of free society and work to create, care, comfort, educate, and encourage the arts, to provide opportunity, and to enhance health and well-being where it is found wanting.

> *The mission says why you do what you do, not the means by which you do it.*
>
> –Peter Drucker

Most nonprofits are small and focus on one narrowly defined community and issue. Many of them have roots in religious or moral convictions. All of them have a sense that the work they do will result in a benefit for people, a healthier community, a better society, and a more humane world.

Nonprofit organizations, we know, are not about making money for owners or shareholders. And, while they may have influence, they are also not responsible for creating rules or regulations that help structure the way we live together in society.

Nonprofits support and encourage voluntary participation in the highest and best qualities of life in an open society: education, spirituality, legislative advocacy, health and well-being, the arts, sports, the environment, and leisure activities. Forming and promoting a nonprofit means defining the space it occupies in the fabric of that society.

Quite often I hear my nonprofit management students say that they are taking graduate nonprofit courses so they can someday open "their own" nonprofit organizations. I quickly challenge them and suggest that a nonprofit is not "owned" by an individual; it is owned by the community. That means that the community must be supportive of the work being done.

Support from the community is usually indicated by the numbers of people and amount of financial support for the organization. Receipt of one or two grants, even large grants, does not constitute broad community support. And one of the reasons that most fundraising consultants advocate for a broad base of individual donor support is because it demonstrates that the organization has a place in the community and a role in society that others will support.

So, consider well the importance of the development and effective continuation of an organization of the social sector. It cannot be understated.

Voluntarily Supporting a Mission

The nonprofit sector is often referred to as the voluntary sector for good reason. The organizations that comprise it are all associations of people voluntarily gathering around a common cause. The governance component of the organization is legally mandated to be voluntary and must derive no financial benefit from participation. Additionally, most organizations thrive on a group of hard-working individuals who willingly and voluntarily contribute resources of their time, talents, and treasure to support the organization's work.

Volunteers gather to make their community and the world a better place. They rally under a banner that identifies the cause for which they share their time, energy, resource, finances, and in some cases, even their lifeblood. They work for something greater than the here and now. These people give for the children, the future, and the opportunity to participate in making or remaking their community and world.

It serves the organization and community well if the mission is clear. While the true mission of your organization is bigger than your mission statement, and hard as it is to capture that mission in a few words, it is critical to do so. It is your identity, your purpose, and your reason for existence. It tells the community what you do, with whom you work, and to a degree, the way you accomplish your benefit to humanity.

The challenge of a mission statement is to succinctly capture the essence of your organization in a way that almost instantly communicates who you are and what you do to a complete stranger. When people introduce themselves to new acquaintances as plumbers, auto mechanics, real estate agents, stockbrokers, veterinarians, or physics professors, and they share where they work, those new acquaintances have a pretty good idea of what those people do when leaving home in the morning.

The same should be true of your mission statement. It should tell, in a concise and crisp fashion, about the work you do.

An organization's mission, its long-term vision, and the values under which it operates are so critical that it is hard to conceive of a book about nonprofit leadership and management beginning anywhere else. So, before we consider the sayings and how deadly they are, we need to identify and investigate the basis on which your organization is founded. Who are you and what do you do? Take a look at your organization's mission, vision, and values and an introduction to the seven sayings.

It is almost trite, and perhaps too easy, to say that the mission of the organization is critical. Trite, because it is advocated by so many. Too easy, because it is hard work to state your mission in both a succinct and an understandable way and harder still to stay true to that mission once stated. But that mission statement, as well as the passion and energy behind it, is vital to a nonprofit's survival and success. The mission is what you do and, to a degree, who you work with, how you do it, and where you do it. Now, compress all that into a few words that will fit on a bumper sticker or T-shirt. The mission is what gets you to work every morning and sometimes keeps you awake at night. It is what empowers you, raises your blood pressure, and both gives you energy and saps your strength. It is the "who you are" in your community and among your peers.

> **Mission** refers to what you do and why you exist. The mission statement is the brief articulation of that mission in written fashion. If you have to explain your mission statement to a stranger who has just read it, you have not articulated it well enough.
>
> **definition**

The Vision... View of the Ideal

The vision is just as important as the mission in terms of where you as an organization want to be. What is your end result? Where are you going? Not ethereal, not presumptive, but challenging. Close your eyes and you can see it. Sleep and you dream it. Your vision is that Northern Star in the night sky that leads and pulls you ever on to be the best. Everyone has a vision. No two visions are the same. The only way to make sure that everyone in your organization has a unified vision is to develop it, agree on it, and point to it regularly. Like your mission, it has to be a living, breathing statement. If it grows stale, it needs to be revitalized. Treasure it and let it guide you.

Looking *toward* the future is different from looking *into* the future. The first is having a vision. The second is not within the realm of human capability. A vision of where you want to be as an organization is necessary and compelling. Where are you going as an organization? What do you envision, picture, and see as the end result for your work?

Make sure that everyone in your organization has the same vision by making it a part of your organization's culture. Like your mission, it has to be a confirmation of your direction and intent. If your vision is no longer guiding your staff and volunteers, revisit what it means. Make it truly something that everyone associated with the organization can look toward in the future.

> **Polaris**
>
> The guiding Northern Star for your organization is its vision. It is the drinking gourd your staff and volunteers use to keep working on the mission every day. Seeing the vision coming to fruition makes the hard work meaningful.
>
> **observation**

What Values Do You Hold?

In the process of getting where you want to go, you will need to be true to yourself and others. The principles and values you hold and uphold will determine what sort of a nonprofit you are. They tell the community, your clients, and stakeholders about the quality, the essence, of your being and personality. They guide your interactions with clients and your reactions to donors and stakeholders. They are the way you work together on your mission and toward your vision.

They must be sincere and embedded. Your values are nonnegotiable. They define you. Be true to them.

When considering your organizational values, it is appropriate to consider how you engage with others. The Golden Rule, "Do unto others as you would have them do unto you," is in some aspects rather selfish and self-centered. Perhaps in establishing your organizational values, you might consider an alternate, the Platinum Rule: "Treat others as *they* wish to be treated."

Regardless of size or stature, each organization needs to answer some simple questions and put a stake in the ground about its values before it can move on to accomplish great things. These values are statements of sincerity and intent as well as position and purpose. They should not be overlooked by mature organizations that may believe themselves beyond such mundane things. Nor should they be skipped by young organizations that are investing their energy and enthusiasm into getting programs operational.

> *When your values are clear to you, making decisions becomes easier.*
>
> –Roy E. Disney (1930–2009), Senior Executive, Walt Disney Company

Questions about Mission, Vision, and Values—Your Role in Society

All organizations, be they business, government, or nonprofit, play a role in our democratic culture and way of life. Thinking about the place in our society occupied by your organization, you might ask some of the following questions:

- What is the unique position you occupy in your community?
- What is it that you hope to accomplish for good?
- Has the community embraced what you do and the way you go about doing it?
- Is the vision of the organization's future shared by all staff and stakeholders?
- Does everyone in the organization have a sense of the purpose and theory of change that you promote?
- Can everyone on your board and staff articulate the reason (the mission) for the existence of the organization?

The following is a list of potential practices, processes, actions, and opportunities in a nonprofit organization that relate to the mission/vision/values of that organization. They are captured within the level/symbol where they most appropriately fit along a continuum of legal requirements to excellent practices. Determine your adherence to the practice or action with a check in the box.

🛑 STOP   Red–Stop (Legal Requirements)

✓	Practice or Action
	The organization's founders included a statement of purpose when they filed the articles of incorporation with your state's attorney general or other governmental entity.
	The organization meets all legal requirements for incorporation and continuation of its existence.
	The organization files appropriate documentation, as required with state and federal agencies, and complies with charitable registration laws in a timely fashion.

If your organization has not accomplished the above items, it is possible it is still in the process of becoming a bona fide legal entity or may be "operating without a license." If you are not sure about those responses, now is the time to stop and check. Having your mission articulated and available to the public is critical, and from its inception, it is expected that any nonprofit organization meet all legal requirements for incorporation and work in its jurisdiction.

From the outset, a nonprofit must file annually with state and federal agencies and comply with charitable registration laws. At that point, you should be able to accept donations and carry out business within your state.

Obtaining your 501(c)(3) status from the Internal Revenue Service is the necessary requirement before you are able to provide your donor with a receipt to use to take a tax deduction for a charitable gift. Getting that IRS determination letter is sometimes a lengthy process.

If you are just beginning your work, another solution you might consider is having another nonprofit 501(c)(3) organization serve as your fiscal agent. Both organizations need to share a similar mission and understand the legal ramifications of the relationship. An agreement of this nature allows for a young organization to work on developing its mission, programs, and donors without the initial concerns about the legal and accounting considerations. Later, you may choose to incorporate and file for your own nonprofit tax status. In the meantime, the fiscal agent manages the finances, provides the tax status, issues donor receipts, and generally provides that legal and administrative component to the new nonprofit.

Usually a financial or contracted relationship is established to cover the costs of this service that are incurred by the fiscal agent on behalf of the new organization. Quite often these costs are considerably less than the cost of beginning and setting up new processes and procedures, insurance, banking, etc. It is a consideration worth investigating, but do so following legal advice.

CAUTION — Yellow–Caution (Principled Ethics and Transparency)

✓	Practice or Action
	The mission and work of the organization is supported by members of the community beyond the initial founders.
	The organization has a written mission statement that is articulate, succinct and specific.
	The mission statement clearly identifies the purpose of the organization, the clientele it serves, and the outcomes it expects to have.
	The organization understands the unique position it occupies in the community and is not replicating services already provided. It understands and articulates the work it needs and wants to do.
	The mission and work of the organization is transparent and open to new participants and community input.
	New donors are supporting the work of the organization.
	The organization is having success at recruiting new members to its board and volunteer base.

Many nonprofits develop because of the interest or life experience of one person or a small group of caring and committed individuals. This is neither good nor bad; it's simply the way it happens. Similarly, many businesses develop and grow because of the good idea of one or a few people.

The difference between for-profit and nonprofit organizations now begins to show when the community starts to look at what is going on. While a business can be private and does not need to disclose its financial position in order to continue to provide products and services, the nonprofit organization is public from the beginning and needs to look beyond the customer and client to the community for ongoing support. Nonprofits are "owned" by the community and need to be responsive to that.

So, the ethical and transparency issues of the caution level are concerned with the embracing of the mission and the vision of the organization by the larger community. As noted, the indicators of community support are seen in new and increased contributions, new and more volunteers, and community awareness.

If these signs are not evident for your nonprofit, take a fresh look at the need within the community for your program. Sometimes it is better to acknowledge a lack of support for an idea and partner with another organization than to fight on independently.

Chapter Three

🚦 GO — Green–Go (Good Work/Growing Capacity)

✓	Practice or Action
	The mission statement is known and agreed to by all people in the organization.
	The mission is used to direct and guide the goals and activities of the organization.
	There is a direct correlation between the message used for soliciting funding and the organization's stated mission.
	The board reviews the mission of the organization on a regular (annual) basis and ascertains that the work being accomplished in the organization fits within that mission.
	Staff and volunteers understand how the programs and work they do fits within the organizational mission.
	The organization has clarified a future vision for the organization and its impact on the community it serves.
	The mission, vision, and values are stated clearly and prominently displayed, including in marketing, media, and programmatic communications.
	The core values are espoused by the entire organization, embraced by all its staff and volunteers and are clearly articulated, supported, and demonstrated.

At this point in the life of a nonprofit, the mission, vision, and values are evident, well articulated, known, prominently displayed, and understood by the community.

The mission may have been revised. In addition to a solid mission, there is a sense of future for the organization that finds voice in a stated vision. The vision is accepted and understood.

The organization has also established a set of core values by which it operates and engages with clients and the community.

The importance of the mission, vision, and values is not taken lightly by organizational leaders or staff. They are communicated frequently and discussed often.

🏅 Blue Ribbon (Superior Quality)

✓	Practice or Action
	Job descriptions and performance evaluations demonstrate a connection to the accomplishment of the mission of the organization, including individual appraisal and responsibility for working toward mission objectives.

✓	Practice or Action
	The organization identifies and cooperates with organizations providing similar or complimentary services in the community for the most effective utilization of community resources.
	The mission, vision, and values are reviewed annually and revised as necessary to meet community and organizational needs.
	Marketing and communication messages and materials reflect the mission and values of the organization.
	Staff, board, and other volunteers are expected to uphold the values of the organization in all internal and external representations of the organization.

The mission, vision, and values are a solid part of the organization and its marketing and reporting focus. They are reviewed regularly for their philosophical approach and intent as well as their effective implementation in the organization. At this level, the mission, vision, and values have found their way into job descriptions and evaluation practices. There is good understanding on the part of all stakeholders about the position the organization occupies in the community and the void that would be left if the organization would cease to exist.

Gold Cup (Preeminent Practice/Excellence)

✓	Practice or Action
	The organization openly seeks collaborative partnerships and strategic alliances as a means of advancing their mission and for the benefit of the community.
	The organization seeks to open and maintain channels of communication and understanding between themselves and the public and private sectors in order to best serve community needs.
	The organization understands the unique role nonprofit organizations play in the democratic process and both advocates on behalf of its mission and encourages its membership to actively engage in that process.
	Staff or volunteers may have been or would be warned or disciplined for violations of the organization's stated values.

In order to achieve this level, all of the issues listed in all previous categories must be thoroughly achieved. There is regular reference in publications and printed materials to the mission, vision, and values, and they are discussed openly and honestly within and outside of the organization. Board members and fundraisers regularly discuss and make decisions on the basis of the mission, vision, and values. Other community groups understand the organization's mission and see how the vision and values support that mission. Not only are these reviewed annually, but they are also succinct, memorable, and meaningful. Concerted effort has gone into making them viable as branding, marketing, and communication tools.

The mission is prominently and proudly displayed and communicated; staff and stakeholders know it well and appreciate all it represents. All programming and most income generated fits well under the mission umbrella and is directly affiliated with accomplishing it. New revenue opportunities are discussed against the foundations of the mission, vision, and values. There is a zeal and passion for the mission's accomplishment that is palpable within the organization. The organization publicly and proudly displays its mission as a vital component of the quality of life for the community.

The vision that sets the stage for future planning is believable, and stakeholders expect that it will be achieved. Staff understands how their work moves the organization to attainment of the vision and that it will take a team effort to reach it. Everyone in the organization has a sense of the purpose and "meaning making" that is happening. Collaborative relationships exist with other organizations of the community, including business and government, to support the mission work of the organization.

The organizational values are embedded in the psyche of the stakeholders and in the work that gets accomplished. The values are evident to a visitor, a client, a donor, an evaluator, or anyone who comes in contact with the organization or its people. They are used in determining approaches to work and requests for funding. The mission, vision, and values are contained and referenced in the performance evaluations of staff and volunteers. It is conceivable that a staff member or volunteer has been disciplined for not adhering to organizational values.

At this level, other organizations are seeking guidance from senior leadership about developing and adhering to a mission, vision, and set of values.

Generally, before asking people a bunch of questions about their personal lives, it is appropriate to know who they are, what they do, and something about what they consider important in life. That is what your organization's mission, vision, and values do. They tell the world about who you are, how you are attempting to change your corner of the world, and what your goals are for accomplishing those changes. Without this information, the seven sayings are very difficult to discuss.

To Recap

- Your organization's mission and mission statement are critical to keeping your focus.

- A unified vision of your nonprofit's future will point leadership and management in the same direction.

- Your organization's values will let your clients and your communities see what makes you worth their support.

- Determining and defining your organizational role in society will also make you a more valuable community commodity without replicating what is being done by others.

Chapter Four

Deadly Saying One: "Who's In Charge around Here Anyway?"

IN THIS CHAPTER

- Leadership in practice
- Defining differences in leadership
- Questions of leadership practice and quality
- Crossing category boundaries

If the question "Who's in charge?" is being asked, there is uncertainty about who is leading the organization and who is following. While there are different kinds of leadership, there cannot be a void in this function. The following anecdotes, stories, and accounts ask questions of leadership and responsibility.

Whose Permission Do I Need?

Amanda was standing in the kitchenette with the other program director, John, making another pot of coffee. She was irritated about the news from the board meeting last night. She had asked Susan, the executive director, about sending a survey to the people in her program to determine their satisfaction with the program's services. Susan was afraid that the survey might raise more questions and perhaps cause doubts in the minds of a major funder of this program.

Susan said, "I'll ask the board members what they think and get back to you after the meeting." Early that morning, Amanda had asked Susan about the board's reaction to the survey and questions.

"They weren't against the survey, per se," Susan responded. "What they wanted was more information about how it was going to be disseminated and who would see the results. The treasurer was also wondering about the cost."

"So," Susan continued, "I can't really authorize the survey until we have some more information. The board will want to see a more detailed report next month. Let's take the draft survey to them with all the other information and we'll see after that."

"John, I'm really frustrated," Amanda complained. "I don't know what I can do in the program, or what I need to get Susan's permission for, or what needs to go to the board."

"I know," John replied. "Sometimes you really wonder who is in charge around here anyway!"

It Is Just Business as Usual

As a newly elected board member, Gene didn't want to make any waves. However, this was his sixth monthly meeting—he missed one because of an unexpected business trip—and he was still a bit confused. He was drawn to the mission and had been a donor for more than four years. His kids had been involved in one of the summer programs, and he believed the organization had great potential to contribute to his small-town community. Most of the other board members had been with the organization since its founding twelve years ago. As a local attorney, Gene was invited to join the board when one of the founding board members retired and moved out of town.

He was beginning to wonder, however. There did not seem to be any order to the meetings; the board chair had been at only one meeting so far, and Taryl, the executive director, pretty much ran the meetings. The part-time bookkeeper gave the treasurer's report, and except for his five-minute appearance, there were no staff members in attendance.

The major discussion this evening was about the extension of contracts for food and supplies for the summer camp. Taryl had submitted the list of recommended providers. While there were no comparative bids, the board members seemed okay with the same group of providers they had used the past several years, with one exception. The vice chair, Kathy, had heard that the owner of Sander's Food Service was being questioned about some hiring practices and might be indicted on federal employment violations. She wanted to hold off with that particular contract until the investigation was completed.

Taryl jumped in: "I've known Tom Sanders for years. This is just business as usual. We've used his food service for almost a decade, and he gives us a good price. I don't have time to look for another bid. We need this contract signed now. Would someone please make a motion to accept all the bids just as I presented them?"

Gene finally spoke up. "Wait just a minute," he cautioned. "This is not something to take lightly. We need to protect our reputation and our clients. If there is a potential down side, we should wait. And, by the way, just who is in charge around here anyway?"

Strategic or Not?

It had been a particularly trying afternoon. Sue, the longtime program director for Operation Access, had a meeting scheduled with Fred, the newly appointed chair of the board's program committee. Unsure of the agenda for the meeting, Sue had invited her executive director, Janice, to join them.

Fred began the meeting by emphasizing the need for new and innovative programming to meet the needs of the clients and the community. He questioned Sue about the direction in which Operation Access was headed and how she was implementing new and different ideas into the activities. This was, he believed, his responsibility after all. He was known for his business acumen and ability to turn around failing operations. Innovation was his passion, and as a new board member and recently appointed chair of the program committee, he believed it was his job to infuse new ideas into the worn-out operations of the organization.

Before Sue got a chance to tell Fred about the recent innovations in the program and changes over the last few years, Janice jumped in. "Fred, please understand. We have the direction in our strategic plan to work on program cost containment this year. The new three-year strategic plan was approved at a meeting before you came on the board. We aren't planning any new or innovative programming until we have done everything we can to increase the cost-benefit ratios of our current programming. We have plans to add new programming, but not until next year."

"But innovation is the name of the game," Fred countered. "Without constant innovation and new ideas, we will be losing ground. We need to make some changes in this program and soon."

"No," Janice defended, "not right now. We don't have the staffing or budget to handle program innovations right now."

While the disagreement continued with no discernible end, Sue sat in silence watching. Finally, Janice needed to leave to attend to some other issues, and the debate was postponed until the following week when it would be discussed again with the board chair in attendance.

Sue went back to her desk, plopped down in her chair, and in a frustrated and audible whisper said to nobody in particular, "So just who is really in charge around here anyway?"

Questions about Leadership

So as you think about the leadership of your organization (perhaps you are thinking about yourself), the following questions may have been ones you already asked:

- Does our leadership pay attention to the critically important things like the mission, vision, and values?

- How does our board of directors govern the organization? Is it actively engaged, effective, and efficient? Does the board seek to micromanage?

- Are the roles and responsibilities of the various leadership types—board, executive, and management—clearly distinguished, separated, and yet working collaboratively and symbiotically in our organization?

- How does communication from leadership to the rest of our organization happen? Is it frequent and effective?

- Is the diversity of our community represented in our organizational leadership and is our leadership represented in the community? Do we contribute to our community as well as ask it to contribute to us?

- Do our leaders advocate for our cause and encourage others to do the same?

Leadership in Practice

This first deadly saying asks about leadership. Not in the theoretical or philosophical sense, as an introspective, or as a "be a better leader" recipe book. It is about leaders *doing* things that leaders need to do. An organization cannot exist without leadership. Every organism needs a head in order to live and function. In the case of a nonprofit organization, there are at least three types of leadership: governing leadership, executive leadership, and managerial leadership. They all need to work. They need to work together and at times independently, but they all need to work. If one of them is not working, the others may try to pick up the slack. But that can be only a short-term solution. The challenge is often about who is actually in charge and leading.

The reason that a deadly saying, or question, about leadership is the first, following closely after mission, vision, and values, is because of the critical importance that leadership is to your nonprofit organization's effectiveness. While there are many ways an organization can die, the quickest, surest, and usually most painful is through poor leadership.

Is There a Leader in the House?

There was a popular folk trio back in the 1960s who asked a question that might be paraphrased like this:

Where have all the leaders gone?
Long time passing…

Where have all the leaders gone?
Long time ago…

Where have all the leaders gone?
Gone to seminars, everyone…

When will they ever return?
Oh when will they e'er return?

So, even with everything about leadership that has been written about, "seminared" about, blogged about, or tweeted about, we still sometimes wonder who is in charge? Is it the board?

Is it the executive director? Perhaps it is the receptionist, who sometimes appears to be the only one actually working.

Leadership is hard work. It is easier to ignore an issue with the hope that it will fix itself or just go away than have to deal with it. However, we know that is not likely to happen.

This chapter will ask you to think about the things you do or do not do that are important for leaders of a nonprofit organization to undertake. The intent is to concentrate on actions and practices that are legally required, are expected, or are good or better practices of leadership and governance.

Defining Leaders and Leadership Types

For clarity of discussion here, "key" or "critical" leaders include the executive director or chief executive officer and those staff members who report directly to the CEO. Staff refers to program staff or volunteer workers with direct relationships to clients or service participants. In many cases, there will be overlap in these leadership categories. In a small organization, the executive director may be directly serving clients alongside of members of the board of directors.

> Governance, executive, and managerial leadership are all important components of organizational leadership. They each serve different functions, but they must work symbiotically to accomplish the mission.
>
> **observation**

This discussion and the descriptions of some of these actions differentiate among three types of leadership. First is the leadership that is most appropriately called governance, which rests in the volunteer board of directors. This is where the ultimate legal responsibility for the organization resides. The voluntary members of the board of directors come from the community and are accountable to that community for the actions of the organization. This concept is both theoretical and practical. It is designed to be so in response to the government's waiving of tax payments on some revenue and the ability of the organization to accept tax-deductible contributions from donors.

Secondly, there is executive leadership, normally delegated to the executive director or CEO. This person is ultimately responsible for implementing the strategy and directing the organization. The executive director hires the staff and upholds the policies as directed by the board. While the executive director may hold an *ex officio* (by right of office) position on the board, the executive director generally should not be a voting member of the board. The executive director reports to the board while working in consort to uphold and advance the organization's mission, vision, and values.

Finally, there is managerial leadership, residing in staff or volunteers who have responsibility for directing or managing program components of the organization. It refers to someone with responsibility for day-to-day operational responsibility for a program or service component of the organization. This person may or may not be considered a key leader and might or might not have staff or volunteers who report to the staff member. This person most likely has some direct contact with clients or customers. This staff person is critical to the operation and mission accomplishment of the organization. Just because it is listed third does not make it less important.

All these different aspects of leadership must work together to accomplish the mission of the nonprofit organization. Understanding the different roles and responsibilities along with sound and effective communication practices between leaders and staff is critical to good organizational governance, leadership, and management.

None of these components of leadership is better than any other forms of leadership. Each is special and has a set of activities and practices unique and reserved for that entity.

You will need to determine when, in each situation, people are acting in different leadership capacities. Often, especially in small organizations, board members also serve as direct-service volunteers. In some situations, past or present recipients of the organization's services are also board members. These situations can present challenges to the segregation of duties and responsibilities. It requires great skill to help board members stay focused on the big picture and issues of strategy and policy when their tendency is to view the organization through their position as a direct service volunteer.

It is up to you to make the terminology and concepts fit your organizational structure. It will also behoove you to determine when, in such a situation, people are acting in different capacities. When in the boardroom, a board member needs to focus, think, and act differently from when that person is working in a program as a volunteer serving the clients.

> Key leaders are defined as the executive director or chief executive officer and those who report directly to the CEO. Staff refers to program staff or volunteer workers with direct relationships to clients or service participants.
>
> definition

Crossing Category Boundaries

It may seem like you have reacted to similar questions and activities in the previous chapter on mission that are considered again in this one on leadership. You are right. There are commonalities yet subtle differences. Having a mission statement is different from governing leaders paying attention to the mission statement when they make decisions. So, consider the relationships between chapters and between the deadly sayings of the book. You will find some interesting relationships and connections.

The following is a list of potential leadership practices, processes, actions, and opportunities in a nonprofit organization. Each line item is captured within the level/symbol where it most appropriately fits along a continuum of legal requirements to excellent practices. Determine your adherence to the practice or action with a check in the box.

STOP Red–Stop (Legal Requirements)

✓	Practice or Action
	The official documents of our organization, such as the articles of incorporation, bylaws, accounting records, tax filings, and board meeting minutes, are available for the scrutiny of members and other stakeholders who want to inspect them for a proper purpose.
	The board meets at least four times (preferably more) a year with a quorum in attendance.
	The members of the board of directors are familiar with and review on a regular basis the official documents of our organization, such as the articles of incorporation, bylaws, accounting records, tax filings, and minutes.
	The board of directors takes action to ensure the accuracy of our organization's financial records. This is accomplished through engagement of an outside auditor or other means to ensure proper internal financial control.
	An independent professional financial audit is required for any organization when annual revenues exceed $750,000. We adhere to that requirement.
	The officers of the board of directors are, at the minimum, a chair and treasurer—plus a vice chair and secretary as appropriate.
	No one person holds two offices on the board simultaneously.
	The executive director, if a voting member of the board of directors, does not hold an officer position.
	The board approves an annual budget for the operation of our organization and reviews actual revenues and expenses in relation to the budget on a regular and systematic basis.
	The board has a process in place to ensure the proper and timely filing of all required tax filings, financial reports, and registrations.
	The board regularly reviews and verifies the accuracy of our organization's records and accounts.
	Members of our board of directors serve voluntarily in that capacity and are compensated only for reasonable travel or other expenses related to their service.
	The board of directors ensures management of our organization's property and finances in a way that is consistent with the intent of our donors' restrictions, prudent judgment, and sound management practice.
	Members of the board understand and regularly review the requirements of state and federal statutes as they pertain to our organization. This is especially true with regard to solicitations, sales and income taxes, and unemployment and workers' compensation obligations.

> **Ex officio** means "by right of office" and usually refers to the position of executive director or chief executive officer as a member of the board of directors. While this position is appropriate, it is considered good practice for the executive director or CEO not to be a *voting* member of that board, or if so, that person should not hold the position of an officer of the board. This is different from the private sector, where the CEO is often also the chair of the board.
>
> — definition

If your organization is fairly new or very small, you might find some inconsistencies or items missing from the above list of legal expectations. If you find there are things in the Red-Stop category that you and your board are not doing, pay attention to the basics of good governance. Failure to have basic policies and practices in place can result in legal problems or administrative actions against your organization.

Beyond those governance legalities, pay attention to your finances. Do not take anything for granted. Write out policies and procedures and follow them.

If you are unsure about how to develop or word some of the policies around solid governance and finance, you can do a couple of things:

- Ask your state association of nonprofit organizations or a statewide or national watchdog group for suggestions.

- Investigate sample policies and procedures from online libraries, universities, or management organizations.

- Ask another organization, one that's well managed, to share its policies, practices, and procedures. Be cautious with this, however, because it also may be operating with flawed information.

- Check with knowledgeable nonprofit legal counsel for assistance.

One of my graduate students is currently developing the case studies of several nonprofit organizations in a small town where one person, a board member of each of the organizations, absconded with funds from all of them. This person was also the pastor of a local church.

Everyone trusted the pastor and others around the board table. There did not appear to be a need for financial policies or fiscal accountability. Now both the town and these organizations are suffering. Worse, their clients are suffering and will do so for some time because donors to these local organizations are very apprehensive and cautious about continuing to donate, knowing that their previous donations were not well stewarded.

Now let's take a look at those practices and expectations of leadership that are more about ethics and organizational transparency. You might argue that some of these are legally required. Depending on the type of client you serve or the geography within which you work, some of them may have legal requirements. In most cases, these fit the "should do" rather than the absolute "must do" category of practice.

⚠ CAUTION Yellow–Caution (Principled Ethics and Transparency)

✓	Practice or Action
	Our board of directors and executive leaders are identified publicly and they communicate regularly with the community and the public served by our organization.
	Paid staff members do not serve on the board of directors as voting members. The executive director or CEO may serve on the board in an ex officio capacity with voice but no vote.
	Meeting minutes are recorded at every board meeting by our secretary or a designee. They reflect both the actions taken and the discussion that led to those actions.
	The minutes of the meetings of the board of directors are retained in an official repository and are distributed to our board members for their review and acceptance.
	Members of our board of directors regularly stand for reelection to office. Bylaws set a limit on the number of consecutive terms or total years served by any board member... generally a maximum of nine or ten consecutive years.
	The members of our board of directors take seriously their responsibility for assisting our organization to obtain adequate financial and other resources to execute its charitably purpose and mission.
	The board of directors takes appropriate action to ensure proper internal controls for the finances and property of our organization. These controls include separated responsibilities and authority for deposit and withdrawal of funds, consummation of contractual obligations, payment of bills and solicitation, and acceptance of donations.
	The board of directors has established policies and mandated practices for the privacy and security of all client, customer, and stakeholder data and for the retention and subsequent destruction of the official financial and legal documents of the organization as appropriate.
	The board of directors has established policies and mandated practices to ensure that our donor records are private and are not sold or given to other organizations.
	The board of directors and key leaders promote and encourage ethical and legal behavior at all levels in the organization. Their actions model and support the organizational values. They promote self-discipline and are not afraid to call their own members to account for their actions as public representatives of the organization.
	Our organization has a written conflict-of-interest policy and effective practice for avoiding conflicts of interest that may arise. We regularly request that all members of the board of directors and key staff agree to and sign the policy statement.

Advancing beyond this category suggests that you have minimally accomplished your legal requirements and have some other positive practices in place. Make sure that your organization is accomplishing all the basic standards expected by accrediting agencies, auditors, and watchdog organizations.

Look at the expectations of the Association of Fundraising Professionals, the Better Business Bureau, or any state or regional watchdog-type organization for recommendations about the most important of these issues. These will provide direction on fiscal accountability, segregation of governance and leadership duties, financial accountability, donor stewardship, and practical recommendations for transparency to the larger community.

Now is the time to begin to move practices beyond the "we need to do that sometime" and have the necessary discussion, commit policy and procedure to paper, and enforce their authority throughout the organization. Spend time as well to work toward full board involvement and regular participation in board meetings and fundraising endeavors. The members of your board represent the community. If they are not loyal, caring, and obedient to the organization and do not support proper legal and ethical issues, it is unlikely that others in the community will be supportive.

GO Green–Go (Good Work/Growing Capacity)

✓	Practice or Action
	Key leaders communicate regularly and effectively to and with all staff, volunteers, donors, and members of our organization.
	Leadership ensures that the mission statement of our organization is clear, succinct, and reviewed on a regular basis for accuracy and relevance.
	Our organization has determined a vision for the future of the organization and leadership calls organizational attention to the vision on a regular basis.
	Our organization has developed a set of values and leadership ensures that all staff, volunteers, and stakeholders of the organization are committed to those values as guides for their work.
	The board of directors and key leaders ensure that all staff, volunteers, stakeholders, and the community understand the mission, vision, and values of our organization. These efforts take multiple and varied paths to accomplish this goal and include both marketing and fundraising endeavors along with programming decisions.
	The members of our board of directors are active in the governance of the organization by attending and participating at meetings and by reading and understanding the minutes and reports.
	Our board of directors and key leaders encourage and provide opportunity for two-way communication with and among the board, staff, volunteers, clients, and stakeholders of the organization. They really listen to what staff and stakeholders have to say.
	Our board of directors and leadership advocate publicly and passionately for our cause and encourage others to do the same.
	The qualifications, expectations, and responsibilities of the members of the board of directors are clearly identified in written documents and job descriptions. The expectations for board involvement and responsibilities are clear and understood by the entire board.

✓	Practice or Action
	New members of the board are provided with a job description and an orientation, including a review of the board roles and responsibilities.
	The board of directors establishes committees as needed to inform or report to the board, regularly scrutinizes the committee's work, and disbands the committee when its service is complete.
	Formal actions taken by the board of directors at a legally called meeting of the board are not routinely revisited or regularly overturned at a subsequent meeting.
	Members of the board of directors take seriously any reports of officer, leader, or staff mismanagement, theft, misconduct, or illegal activity and act immediately to ascertain the validity of such reports. They report such information to appropriate authorities as required by law.
	The board of directors engages outside legal, financial, fundraising, and/or management counsel as appropriate and necessary for the effective and efficient operation of the organization and to educate itself on best nonprofit practice.
	The board has established a "whistle-blower" policy and process of reporting suspicious activity along with assurances of nonreprisal for such action.
	Procedures are in place at our organization to ensure the anonymity of any donor who wishes so to remain.
	The board of directors is of a size that makes for effective governance based on the mission and size of our organization. Generally, the board should consist of no fewer than seven members in order to encourage broad and effective governance. Larger boards of directors (fifteen-plus members) operate and lead differently from smaller governance entities and require special leadership skills.
	The process for deliberation and agreement upon the evaluation and compensation for the executive director or CEO is documented in meeting minutes of the board. Key leadership compensation is public information.
	Executive compensation in our organization is reasonable and based on market analysis of similar positions, qualifications, and expectations.

Green-Go level is indicated by additional and appropriate work on the definition of leadership responsibilities, practices, and relationship building both within and without the organization. The legal and ethical issues of the previous colors are all in place and functioning routinely. The Green-Go level is about coming into your own as a solid, organized, and thoughtful nonprofit organization.

More than likely, you have some mature governance practices in place and the work of your board and leadership moves smoothly most of the time. Your organization meets the standards of the agencies that watch over nonprofit groups. Legal mandates and regulatory filings are accomplished readily and with little concern about meeting the requirements or timelines.

Now is the time to start embedding some of those better practices into the routine work of the board of directors and the organization. Systematically approaching the review of the mission, vision, and values along with the board policies will help affirm the growth in sound leadership practices. Establishing this review process will also allow important conversation about how to improve and be more effective and efficient.

If you are missing some of the items mentioned above, now is the time for a serious conversation between your board leadership and your executive leadership to determine the best and most expedient ways to accomplish them.

Regular and systematic evaluation of the board and its effectiveness is important for future growth. Spend time reviewing the recruitment of board members, board job descriptions, committee structure, and term limits. Document some of the better practices and evaluate them for their effectiveness.

Spend time as well on the relationship between the board and the executive director. There should be no surprises at the executive director's annual review. Goals and operational targets should be well documented and monitored.

Blue Ribbon (Superior Quality)

✓	Practice or Action
	All the members of our board of directors make personal financial contributions of substance in addition to their time commitment to the organization.
	The conflict-of-interest policy is reviewed, affirmed, and implemented by all parties on a regular basis.
	The composition of our board of directors and the key leaders reflects the multiple diversities of the community we serve, including ethnic, cultural, financial situation, gender, sexual orientation, age, and other groups impacted by our organization.
	The board annually assesses and evaluates its capacity to govern effectively with a formal evaluative process. It ensures that it is not micromanaging the organization or undermining the executive leadership or, conversely, remaining too distant to effectively establish governance policy for the organization.
	The board of directors has established policies and procedures ensuring nondiscriminatory practices for all demographic categories of legally protected persons as well as setting expectations of behavior in regard to any type of inappropriate behavior or discrimination within the organization.

✓	Practice or Action
	A regular process for reviewing all documents, policies, and practices for improvement, relevance, and compliance is in place and accomplished.
	Clear documentation and regular communication is in place that distinguishes between the responsibilities of governance and those of executive leadership.
	The board of directors sets annual expectations or performance objectives for the organization and for our executive director or CEO.
	The board reviews our CEO's performance expectations against the actual performance of the organization.
	The board and executive leadership regularly seek and participate in learning opportunities that enhance their ability to govern and lead the organization.

The Blue Ribbon category suggests that your leaders are effective, efficient, caring, and loyal. They are running a pretty tight and well-performing organization.

If you have attained most of the items of the Blue Ribbon category, I suspect that the days of putting out fires at the board of directors' meetings are pretty well behind you. Executive leadership works effectively with the board and staff. The challenges at this level are likely to be the embedding of procedures to make sure that there is consistency and regularity in the practices of governance and leadership. Is there regularity of policy review? Are the processes being improved and strengthened each time?

Organizational transparency in your decision-making processes and policy recommendations should be the norm rather than occasional. Your board and executive staff are comfortable encouraging staff and stakeholders to be present at meetings and advocate two-way communications at all levels of the organization.

There may still be some small pockets of resistance on the board or staff that prevent full attainment, and these will be the areas that need to be addressed strategically. A few unwilling or less than enthusiastic board members or a long-held, inappropriate practice may still be holding you back. Look for ways to evaluate the work you are doing and measure success by your growth from one year to the next.

This is also the time to investigate the practices of other excellent organizations. Conversations with their leadership may provide ideas for overcoming one of your deficits and you will certainly have ideas to share with them. Taking time to consider the varied leadership styles and comfort areas of your governance and leadership team will help them to understand the strengths and weaknesses of the team as well as individual contributions to those strengths and weaknesses.

Gold Cup (Preeminent Practice/Excellence)

✓	Practice or Action
	Our organization considers its responsibility to contribute to the well-being of the community in addition to its capacity to receive support from the community. We actively seek ways to support other organizations and causes that contribute to our overall work and mission.
	The members of our board of directors are passionate about the work of the organization. They provide inspiration for the staff and volunteers, and they investigate and recommend innovative practices and opportunities.
	A process for determining the effectiveness of communication at a number of levels throughout our organization is in place. We actively seek input from all levels of the organization and from stakeholders outside our walls.
	Board and executive leaders encourage growth in leadership skill and managerial effectiveness for staff and lead that through personal example.
	We have worked to establish succession plans for key leaders in our organization at both the board of directors and executive levels.
	Our leadership is constantly exploring and advocating for new and innovative ideas. They are regularly seeking opportunities for growth education and learning and encourage the same for others.

If you checked all of these, congratulations and *wow*! It appears that you have high expectations about the quality of leadership in your organization and are diligent about maintaining it. Do not rest on the excellence you have attained. Eternal vigilance and constant attention to improvement and consistency of processes is necessary.

> **observation**
> If your organization received an *unqualified* audit opinion for three or more consecutive years, you get extra credit. If you received a *qualified* opinion in any of the last three years, start asking why. If a legally required audit was not performed, you need to go back to the Red–Stop category.

Continually communicating across leadership segments and levels is necessary so that the reasons for a policy or practice do not get lost in your history. Persistently improving and modifying those policies and governance practice are necessary to meet the challenges of an ever-changing landscape in our nonprofit sector and the larger economic and political uncertainties in which we live.

Succession planning and providing opportunities for education and growth for people at all leadership levels in the organization is a sign of longevity and future prosperity. Recruiting, empowering, and retaining excellent leaders will go far toward the growth and stability of your organization.

So, Who's In Charge around Here Anyway?

I hope that everybody in your organization is in charge of the domain for which that individual's leadership is expected and needed. It takes many different kinds of leaders to operate a nonprofit in these tumultuous times.

It takes governing leaders. It takes leaders who are caring and loyal to your organization and who are equally knowledgeable and obedient to the legalities of operating an important organization of your community. It takes leaders who are not afraid to govern an organization effectively without treading on those leadership aspects ascribed to the executive leader.

If you are one of those governing leaders, take time to contemplate which of the many items noted above are weak or missing from your governance or policymaking practice. Focus on the few most critical items of legal or ethical significance.

In addition, remember that the governance of your organization is a team effort. All members of your board of directors need to engage actively in the work. Governing leadership must also work in tandem with the executive leadership. If it is working well, strive to strengthen it. If it is not, determine the flaws in the relationship and mend them quickly or take the responsibility to move forward for the sake of the community you serve. After all, you are the elected or appointed representatives of that community.

It certainly takes executive leadership in a nonprofit. If you are that leader, you find yourself at the juxtaposition of responsibility to a vision for greater community good and the realities of daily service delivery to your clients and stakeholders. This leadership position is not for the faint of heart. It balances the scrutiny of the community, the demands of stakeholders, and the needs of staff and clients.

> *Leadership is practiced not so much in words as in attitude and in actions.*
>
> –Harold S. Geneen (1910–1997), President of ITT Corporation

Executive leadership must have both heart *and* steely determination. This leader must attend to the personal needs of staff and yet demand absolute best performance from those same people. Executive leaders need to look both inwardly at their own style, attitudes, and expectations and outwardly at the performance of their work team and the processes of accomplishing that work.

In addition, it takes managerial leaders to run a nonprofit. Leaders who have special knowledge of the needs and wants of clients, customers, service recipients, patrons, and stakeholders. Leaders who sometimes need to manage "up" and inform or challenge their executive leaders. Your organization needs leaders who show up day after day and manage the work of your nonprofit.

Leadership is arguably the most important aspect of organizational success. It is required at many levels in a nonprofit and cannot be abdicated if the mission is going to be accomplished.

All of these leadership components must work together to make your work of creating a better place in your community a reality. That is, after all, the reason for your organization's existence, right?

To Recap

- Leadership means practicing being a leader, not just being a leader in theory.

- There are different kinds of leadership in a nonprofit organization, all of which are critical in their practice and impact.

- Leaders need to work together. Governance, executive, and managerial leaders need to work strategically together, not in opposition to each other.

- If your organization is going to get better, pursue effectiveness, or develop a culture of performance excellence, you, the leader, will need to expect it and make it happen.

- Communication is the best tool available for leadership. Practice being a good communicator.

Chapter Five

Deadly Saying Two: "Somehow We'll Get By... We Usually Do!"

IN THIS CHAPTER

- Questions about planning
- Planning to get where?
- Strategic and operational planning
- Establishing goals and tactical activities
- Setting budgets, determining measurements, and assigning responsibilities

Several, including Yogi Berra and a fictitious, philosophical feline from Cheshire, have commented about the importance of the route to get to a destination. It is important to know where you are going and how you plan to get there. More so for an organization that has within itself people with potentially differing ideas about the destination or the way. So when someone in your organization proclaims, "Somehow we'll get by... we usually do!" you can bet that planning has not been an organizational priority. But it should be.

No One Ever Thought...

The phone call from the executive director of the United Way (UW) that morning had been devastating. Donations to UW were down this year, meaning a decrease in total dollars to support children's programming efforts. That was bad enough, but the board of the UW also determined to shift funding priorities to what they believed was a more critically important set of immediate survival needs for at-risk children. The after-school programming Tom's organization provided in three school districts was less critical than food and shelter issues. It would take a 40 percent reduction in funding on top of the reduction imposed due to lack of contributions.

Tom quickly set up a conference call with the members of the board and was now in the process of explaining the situation to them. His director of administration and finance sat across his desk, ready to answer any questions the board might have about the agency finances. The outlook was rather dismal. This was a situation never before encountered. Funding from UW had always been very stable. Oh yes, he had seen fluctuations of a couple of percentage points, but this significant reduction was going to mean the elimination of a significant chunk of programming, if not the whole program entirely. The school districts were suffering themselves and were expected to pull back on their in-kind contributions as well.

Stumbling for answers to his board's queries, Tom felt a lump in his throat. How was he going to explain to staff that at least three, maybe as many as eight, jobs would be eliminated? Why had he not seen this coming? UW funding had been so integral and important, such a big component of their funding. No one ever thought it would drop in half.

Then it was the voice on the phone, the voice of a senior member of the board. "Somehow we'll get by... we usually do!" summed up the deflated spirit of the gathering.

Priorities and More Priorities

The board of directors meeting was well under way. The board had heard the reports of the secretary, the treasurer, the director of development, and the executive director. Even before getting into the old or new business of the agenda, Alex, the board chair, mumbled to himself: "This is going to be a long and interesting evening!"

He went over what had happened so far this evening in his mind. The treasurer's report had looked okay. Not great, but they would not need to use the line of credit at the bank as they had last year at this time. The cutback in staff hours and elimination of the one small program had allowed them to stay above water so far this year.

But the report of the development director did not bode well. The two grants that seemed solid at budget time had been denied. That meant the important program they supported would be in jeopardy in just two months.

The development director also indicated there was a recently released RFP to provide services to a demographic of the community the organization had not dealt with previously. She wanted permission to apply for the funding.

The executive director reported a conversation with a member of the county board of commissioners. The county, it seems, is going to be looking for an organization to handle some of its backlog of clients for six to nine months. "Would our organization be interested in applying to provide this service?" he was wondering.

Just before the beginning of the meeting, Franklin, the longtime chair of the membership committee, had wanted to discuss the revitalization of the membership event. Alex remembered it was cancelled three years earlier after several years of poor participation.

And then there was the issue of the retirement of the executive director. It was less than three months away. The executive director had been at the helm for over ten years... through thick and thin, as it were. What about the party, and her successor?

"Oh well," Alex muttered as the discussion began to get unruly. "Somehow we'll get by. We usually do!"

Helpful... or *Not*?

The staff meeting had gone rather well right up to the last five minutes. It was at that point when Jim, the director of development, asked: "How am I supposed to accomplish any of my fundraising goals when I don't get any support from the rest of the staff?"

"What do you mean?" retorted Fahima, the director of programs,

"Are you referring to my program staff? You've insinuated this before, and I want it made clear that we give you all the information you need to file your grant reports."

"I'm not talking about filing grant reports," Jim countered.

"I'm talking about letting me in on the direction your programs are going. I need to know several months in advance in order to develop and submit a proposal or investigate a prospective donor's interest in supporting a program. Sometimes I don't find out about what you are doing until after you begin providing services, and then you want me to find dollars to support what you've already begun. By that time it is usually too late, but I get blamed for not being a capable fundraiser!"

"I'm sorry you feel that way, Jim" replied Fahima. "I often don't have much warning. Things just come up... opportunities to do more or different work... and I make quick decisions about pursuing them or not. Nobody else has questioned my decisions before. And, except for that problem last year, I've made good ones."

"It's not your decisions I'm questioning, stated Jim. "It is the process and timing of making those decisions. If you pulled me into the loop, I'd be able to help with the funding issues and help you make better decisions about what can be funded by contributions or grants."

"I agree," concurred Stan, the director of administration and operations. "Often those seemingly minor program changes you make cause significant issues of space and client billing. More than once I've had to put on extra staff or authorize overtime to support what seemed like a little change for you."

"And what about marketing?" questioned the director of communications, Chris. "I need time as well to develop appropriate media releases and get the word out. We need to educate our constituents about changes in our services. It doesn't happen overnight."

"You all have valid points and good concerns" interjected Sara, the executive director. "I wish I could offer more than an encouragement to try to work together. I've been after our *board of directors to work with me on developing a strategic, long-range plan since I arrived a year ago. They don't see the need and haven't wanted to expend the energy to do one." The treasurer told me: "As long as we are doing okay financially, we shouldn't rock the boat with too much planning."*

"So try to work it out," concluded Sara. "Somehow we'll get by... we usually do!"

Questions about Planning

- What is the direction our organization will take in the next three to five years?
- Who determined and established that direction, that plan? Was the community involved? Other stakeholders? Staff?
- Does our plan set the groundwork for success, and is it workable and doable?
- Is it truly strategic or simply a repeat of what has always been done?
- Does it take into account our organization's strengths, weaknesses, opportunities, and threats (SWOT)?
- Does it consider the political, economic, social, and technological (PEST) issues confronting the organization?
- Does it look both at the current environment and the future environment?
- Are the goals of our organization specific, measurable, attainable, realistic, and time-bound (SMART)?
- Is there agreement on the tactics for getting that larger plan implemented?
- Are our operational tactics, activities, and timelines tenuous or clearly defined?
- Does staff know what is expected of them, and is there a timeframe for accomplishment?
- Do staff and stakeholders know how their work, activities, and performance fit into the long-range plan of our organization?
- Are staff and volunteers evaluated on the basis of their contribution to the accomplishment of our plan?
- Is the budget based on the plan, or the plan on the budget?

Conducting seat-of-the-pants activities and constantly putting out fires is counterproductive and does not move an organization toward accomplishing its mission. Planning at some level is critical to effectiveness and efficiency in an organization.

Planning

Somebody in your organization has a plan. It may be that everyone in your organization has a plan. It may also be that none of those plans are the same plan. It may well be that different members or segments of your organization, following different plans, are working at cross-purposes and impeding the progress of any of those plans from getting accomplished.

Organizational planning and the implementation or execution of that plan is critical to survival and success. There are many ways to approach planning. This book will not suggest one method as better than another. However, it will ask some important questions about the quality of the process of plan development and implementation of the same.

Planning to Get Where?

Without organizational planning, your success is determined by the thinking of one or two people. Better long-term results are accomplished through involvement of a group of committed and passionate people in determining that goal and direction.

This is particularly true in an organization that has at least two bottom lines (mission and finances) and multiple stakeholder groups (clients, participants, funders, staff, board) to satisfy. You need to know what each of those groups wants and expects.

Strategic planning as a practice originated millennia ago in the military. The etymology of the word strategy is from the Greek verb στρατέγω "to be a general." In other words, think and act like, "be," a military leader. Contemplate how you will win the war. Deliberate the way in which you will be triumphant in the battle. Envision the things you will need to do to accomplish your mission.

When the future of your country and the lives of your soldiers are hanging in the balance, a solid strategy for victory is critical. When the existence of your organization and the lives of your clients are concerned, a good plan is equally important.

As in battle, that plan needs to be strategic. The plan must focus you and your organization in a direction that takes into consideration a variety of environmental factors and the available resources and capacity of your organization to accomplish its mission. It cannot be overly idealistic on one hand, or pessimistic and complacent on the other.

Strategic plans for large organizations are sometimes months in the making and involve many hundreds of hours of work and consulting time. They are extensive and detailed, usually contained in multicolored bound documents of dozens of pages.

Still other, sometimes equally effective, strategic plans have been drawn out on a legal pad over lunch by a couple of key stakeholders, with the cost of sandwiches being the only outlay of cash for the plan.

Neither of these plans is any good if not implemented effectively and efficiently. Operational (sometimes called tactical) planning is a critical component of the strategic plan that is often overlooked or short-shrifted. A good strategic plan is solid only if the organization has the managerial ability to put the tactics and processes in place to accomplish the objectives. This means that the plan needs to be a usable document.

> For the purpose of this book, *goal* and *objective* will be used synonymously, as they are in Webster's and defined as a major initiative of a strategic plan. *Tactic* and *activity* are also, for this discussion, to be understood as the component actions necessary to carry out the goals or objectives.
>
> **definition**

And strategic planning is also challenged if the organizational leaders cannot think and respond strategically to an increasingly changing and tumultuous environment. Planning for the long term is critical, but being able to change those plans because an opportunity presents itself or a threat arises is another component of being able to "*think and act like a general.*"

The following is a list of potential organizational strategy and planning practices, processes, actions, and opportunities in a nonprofit organization. They are captured within the level/symbol where they most appropriately fit along a continuum of legal requirements to excellent practices. Determine your adherence to the practice or action with a check in the box.

🛑 STOP Red–Stop (Legal Requirements)

There are no legal requirements for planning. A nonprofit does not need to report or demonstrate in any compliant way that it has a plan for the future. So doing any sort of planning is a good start.

Of course, your board members need to understand the direction in which your organization is headed in order to meet their legal responsibility to ensure that things are managed well.

If yours is a new organization or one without a plan for the future, do not despair. You are not alone. Many new, forming, or small organizations have begun with an idea and the passion of a founder or small group.

Gather a group of those people who care about your organization along with your vision for the future. Concentrate on clarifying the mission statement and clearly articulating what your organization does and the impact it will have on your community.

Take time to establish a few goals you would like to accomplish in the next couple of years. Use the template at the end of this book to set some basic agreement about the activities you will undertake to accomplish those major goals. Finally, agree to use the plan's format for your ongoing discussion about how you are doing. Focus your attention on the important ideas and strive to get better at planning your future and that of your constituents.

🚦 CAUTION Yellow–Caution (Principled Ethics and Transparency)

✓	Practice or Action
	Your organization has agreed upon and penned a mission statement, organizational vision, and set of values by which the organization will abide.
	The mission statement is clear and succinct and does not require explanation to someone who hears it the first time.
	The mission, vision, and values of your organization are reviewed on a regular basis and communicated to stakeholders and the community.
	Some goal setting or expectations of annual accomplishment are established at the top level of the organization.
	A report is generated on a regular basis that outlines in at least a broad fashion the projected goals and past accomplishments of your organization.

Organizations of the social sector have a relationship and position of responsibility within the community. That position of privilege expects that planning will be accomplished in a manner sufficient for the community to witness and accept. The plan should be tied to the organization's mission and vision for the future. Those goals should be clear and not require a paragraph of explanation.

Ethical issues and those of organizational transparency suggest that minimal standards or expectations for planning are for a regular review of the mission of the organization and a determination that it is still fulfilling a community need.

If you find yourself in this position, the planning template at the end of the book will assist you in putting some basic plans in place.

Your community has a right to expect you are doing some planning for the future and can share those plans with the public that supports and finances your efforts.

🚦 GO Green–Go (Good Work/Growing Capacity)

✓	Practice or Action
	Long-range planning is undertaken on a regular basis by a group of key leaders in our organization.
	The mission, vision, and values are regularly reviewed as a component of our long-range planning to ascertain their continued relevance for the community and current organizational direction. They help focus the organization on serving the needs of our constituents and stakeholders and have a positive impact on the community.

✓	Practice or Action
	The mission statement clearly identifies the purpose of the organization and is used to direct and guide the development of the goals for our organization.
	As an expression of the mission, our organization has agreed upon a future vision for the organization and its impact on the community it serves. This vision aids in the establishment of long-term goals.
	The core values espoused by our organization are embraced by our staff and volunteers and are clearly articulated in the planning agenda and final plan.
	Input from clients, constituents, and community stakeholders is gathered and used as a part of this long-range planning process.
	An assessment of the environment, including investigating the strengths and weaknesses of your organization and the opportunities and threats (SWOT) present in your market is undertaken as part of the planning process.
	An assessment of the current and future political, economic, social, and technological (PEST) or, additionally, environmental and legal (PESTEL) factors relating to the programming, activities, or operations of our organization is considered as a part of the planning process.
	Goals are defined and articulated so that the specific intent is clear and timelines are established for their accomplishment.
	Measures of accomplishment are included and the goals can realistically be accomplished by our organization based on available resources of people, time, and money.
	Goals (or objectives) are written and understood as specific, measurable, acceptable, reasonable, and time-bound (SMART).
	Operational or tactical plans are developed and deployed as part of the process.

At this level, the organization should be publicly stating its goals and objectives for the coming years so that donors and stakeholders have a sense of what their gifts and commitment of resources will support. A solid sense of how those goals and objectives will be realized is also important.

An operational plan should also be in place and routinely used to measure and report on progress toward accomplishing the goals of the strategic plan. Staff and volunteers understand the importance of the strategic plan and see their work as important to attaining the goals stated in that plan.

The challenges at this level are usually to put in place solid data collection and measurement processes to manage toward plan accomplishment. There is often some staff resistance or board member complacency about the importance of data and measurement for decision making.

1st Blue Ribbon (Superior Quality)

✓	Practice or Action
	A formal and disciplined process of developing strategic goals to achieve your organization's mission is undertaken on a regular basis. At a minimum, it is accomplished every three to five years—more frequently as dictated by changing external or internal situations.
	The planning process for your organization includes soliciting and utilizing input from a wide spectrum of constituents, including board members, staff, volunteers, donors; political, religious, cultural, and bureaucratic representatives; and other members of the community as appropriate for your mission and programs.
	The process of planning is regularly reviewed, with the intent of improving the effectiveness and efficiency of the planning process itself.
	The need for programs and services is ascertained through a combination of market research and consultation with other organizations in the community serving similar populations or providing similar services, thereby providing for the most appropriate and nonredundant use of limited community resources.
	Your goals contain an explicit system of measurement and a way of determining when they are achieved or the extent to which they are achievable.
	The board of directors and key leaders unanimously agree on and emphatically support your strategic goals and the activities for achieving them.
	Your organization is comfortable sharing the main strategic objectives with the public to encourage its support of the organization's goals and objectives.
	The strategic goals of your organization are reviewed by key leaders on a regular (minimally annual) basis to determine their continued viability. Revisions are entertained as appropriate to meet changing environmental needs or your organizational capacity.
	An annual operational plan is constructed based on the goals of your strategic plan and provides management and staff with direction for activities, including timelines for completion, appropriate budgets, and responsibility for accomplishment.
	Job descriptions for staff and reviews of staff accomplishments are directly tied to the plan and operational tactics. Everyone has a sense of how their work advances the mission and strategy of the organization.
	The annual plan of operation has a direct tie to your annual budget so that activities that support the accomplishment of the plan have the necessary resources of people, capital, and revenue available for implementation.
	The annual budget is prepared on the basis of organization goals and objectives for the coming year rather than as a reaction to last year's budget.

At this level, regular measurement of actions and tactics has a direct and understandable tie to the accomplishment of the strategic plan. Job descriptions and performance evaluations for staff and volunteers clearly articulate how the everyday work that is accomplished moves the organization closer to the accomplishment of its goals. Staff may have some incentives tied to those same goal accomplishments

Measurements toward goal attainment are internally displayed and made available to the public. Communications from leadership to the organization are often focused on attainment of strategic goals. Regular discussion at the board and senior leadership level is focused on strategic issues, performance, and direction.

The process of accomplishing the strategic plan is also undergoing regular review, and recommendations are being made to make the process more informative and robust.

Gold Cup (Preeminent Practice/Excellence)

✓	Practice or Action
	A measurement system or means of determining achievement of both strategic and operational plans is in place and utilized on a regular basis for reporting of accomplishments to executive leadership, the board of directors, and other key stakeholders.
	Measures of accomplishment of your operational plan are determined based on a number of factors, including benchmarks against other similar organizations, past performance, projected needs, and changes in the market.
	All staff and volunteers know how the work they do impacts the accomplishment of your organizational goals and, hence, your strategic plan.
	Staff understands the expectations of the strategic plan for their job. Performance reviews consider the performance of the individual in relation to individual and team contributions to the goals of your organization.
	The stakeholders of your organization (donors, referents, suppliers, consultants, etc.) understand how their participation and performance impact the ability of the organization to accomplish its goals.
	The strategic planning process is institutionalized and has been regularly improved in some way over the last few years.
	Leaders and staff of your organization understand how important both the process of planning and utilization of the plan itself are to the positive results your organization attains.
	Key suppliers and important stakeholders are encouraged to demonstrate how their contributions to the organization support the organization's goals and objectives.
	Communication about organizational accomplishments toward attainment of strategic goals and applauding individual efforts toward goal realization are regularly shared both internally and with the community and important stakeholders.

I hope that you are sharing your expertise at planning with other, less-adept, groups in your community. The next steps for your organization are probably about improving your ability to predict future trends and opportunities for innovation in your field. Sensing and predicting the needs of constituents and the community is a skill based on much experienced attention to detail. You are also innovating and taking risks. But with a solid planning process, the opportunities provided by innovation in services and products will continue to benefit your clientele.

Planning for what is and what is to come is critical to the functioning and success of your organization. Knowing where you want to go and the direction or path you plan to take makes a big difference in your ability to fulfill your mission and promise to those you serve.

Measuring your performance on the way to accomplishing your plan is a critical piece of success. Being able to effectively manage and lead excellent performance is based on having a solid and accomplishable plan and a functioning tracking system of measures to see how you are attaining that mission and vision.

To Recap

- The importance of developing and implementing strategic and operational planning is critical to an effective organization.

- Establishing and agreeing on major goals/objectives and tactical activities is an important aspect of strategic planning.

- Setting budgets, determining measurements, and assigning responsibilities are significant aspects of strategic and operational planning that are often overlooked.

- Consider using the template in **Appendix C** to assist in developing your strategic goals and operational tactics.

Chapter Six

Deadly Saying Three: "We Know What's Best for Our Clients"

IN THIS CHAPTER

- Listening to your clients
- Questions about client satisfaction
- Why worry about client satisfaction?

Client or customer satisfaction is about more than an annual satisfaction survey. It is about really listening, earnestly, to what your clients and stakeholders are telling you. Your clients and donors are making serious decisions about their money in a challenging economy. Fifty dollars that is not needed to pay rent or bills can go for a theater ticket or a sports ticket, a donation to the food bank or a night out, a children's advocacy campaign or a political action committee. The satisfaction realized and felt by the holder of that fifty dollars will determine where it goes and if it will go there again.

It Is Perfectly Good Food!

The food bank had been inordinately busy. Without any paid staff, it was up to the regular volunteer group to handle everything. The boxes had mostly been packed by another group of volunteers working in the back room. Sue was a new volunteer and was just learning the ropes. She had been assigned to greet people, take down their information, and help them fill out the forms. Agnes, then, would make the determination of the size of the box of food that was to be given away based on family makeup, age of children, and some other factors. The policies were quite clear and had been in place for many years. The boxes were packed ahead. Only so much was given to any client at one time, and exchanges were not allowed unless there was a medical condition. Clients were allowed to "shop" for a few extra items if they were available—things like shampoo or pet food, spices or condiments, and some paper products.

With a line starting to form, Sue was busy trying to help people as best she could, when she heard Agnes say, rather loudly, "What do you mean, you don't want that? It is perfectly good food!"

The client to whom she was speaking rather quietly responded: "Yes, I know that dried peas are good food, but nobody in our house eats them. I thought rather than take them, I'd leave them here for someone else."

"Well!" Agnes snapped as she lifted the peas from the box. "We have lots and lots of dried peas, and they go in every box. They are good for you... make great soup. It is just too bad you don't know how to fix them right."

As Sue turned back to help with the forms, the woman left, looking down so as not to make eye contact with the volunteers or other people in line.

Satisfaction Survey

"At the end of the year, we ask them," responded LaShunda to my question about stakeholder satisfaction.

"Tell me more," I queried.

"Well," she continued, "we send out almost a thousand surveys in December with our holiday letter and end-of-year contribution solicitation. We ask people to respond to a dozen questions to tell us about the service they got and how satisfied they were with the staff."

"I see. What kinds of questions do you ask?"

"Oh, the usual," she responded. "We ask them about how long they had to wait to get seen, how friendly the staff were, whether what we did was helpful or not... things like that."

"And how many surveys do you get back?"

"Oh, we usually get a hundred or so back, and they are almost all good. But we take the comments seriously. Once, when there were some negative comments about not being made to feel welcome, the receptionist got a real talking to by the director. She actually didn't last too long after that."

"Too bad," I said. "So, do you do anything else to find out about how your clients feel? Do you ask them while they are in the program, or maybe at the end of four weeks, when they leave? Do you ask them about anything they gained from the activities?"

"No," LaShunda stated. "That survey is all the county asks us to do, so that is pretty much it. The county tells us what we can do, and we pretty much know what our clients need."

"Even worse," I thought to myself as I walked away and wondered about the use of my tax dollars and their value for the people in the program.

Funder Knows Best

A couple of years after the closing of a nonprofit organization I had come to know, I had the opportunity to meet with a representative of one of that organization's major corporate sponsors. Knowing that their withdrawal of support had been one of the final straws that broke the proverbial camel's back, I asked the sponsor, "Why did you discontinue your contribution to the organization when you did?"

Her answer surprised me. "It wasn't about the money. We could have provided much more. It was all about being seen as a good guy in the eyes of the members. When the membership declined, there was no reason for us to continue. When we finally found out how many members the organization really had... or didn't have, it was an easy decision."

"So, it really wasn't about supporting the work of the organization at all?" I queried.

"Not really," she stated. "It was about having access to the people who associated themselves with the organization. But the leaders never really seemed to care to know why we supported them. They just took it for granted that it was because of the work they were doing. Had they asked, it might have been different. We might have had a different relationship. We might even have helped them rebuild their membership. They thought they knew what we wanted... but never bothered to ask."

Questions about Customer Satisfaction

- Do you really know who your customers/clients/stakeholders are? Are there different groups of them that require different services or products?

- Have you asked your customers/clients/stakeholders about their needs and requirements?

- Are your customers/clients/stakeholders satisfied with the product and services you offer and the manner in which they are delivered? How do you know?

- What have you done to determine changes in those needs and wishes over time?

- Does staff understand what the customers (clients/stakeholders/patrons) want and how best to deliver the product or service to meet those needs?

- Do you investigate what other organizations are doing to meet the needs and expectations of their clients?

Thinking that you know what your clients want and need and actually knowing are two different things. Only one of them uses empirical information from the client's perspective to make that determination.

Nonprofit organizations and their handlers can sometimes be rather arrogant. State and county funds support programming, and the expectations are to provide the service and not ask questions about how to deliver it. Somebody figured out that it would be better to come from our nonprofit than from the county offices, so we just deliver. Clients need to come here to get the service if they want it.

I've heard it expressed that after-school programs are really a help to parents and there isn't any cost to them. What difference is it if the kids aren't too crazy about the activities the staff plans?

> Different segments of the nonprofit community use different terms to describe the people they serve. While I will generally use the term "client" in the text, please replace it with the term's most common equivalent in your organization: customer, student, patient, patron, participant, constituent, or _____ (insert your own term here).
>
> **definition**

It's hard to get great, innovative, and outgoing staff at the pay nonprofits can offer. So the program closes at 5:30, and somebody better be on time to pick up junior!

Job training is about getting someone a job… any job… So "show up and cut your hair!"

"This wetland is critical habitat. Don't you see what you are doing to it? You need to clean it up!"

This attitude is found much too often in our sector. Nonprofit organizations become self-righteous about their relationship with clients and stakeholders. The activities continue pretty much without change each year, and if the number of participants remains at or above previous levels, we figure we're doing just fine.

While the for-profit business community knows that it lives and dies by satisfying its customers, the nonprofit sector sometimes seems to have a sense of overconfidence about its position and relationship with its clients and stakeholders.

Client satisfaction is not the only issue either. Nonprofits must satisfy different and sometimes conflicting groups of folks, and it is difficult to keep their needs separate and distinct. Funders want different things from patrons, and the auditors want something else. Each one needs to be satisfied. And nonprofit leaders sometimes get dizzy trying to keep the requirements for satisfaction or compliance straight.

Why Worry about Satisfaction?

Nonprofit organizations by their very nature serve more than one master. First, they serve the master of their mission and vision. They provide services and products to accomplish the outcomes for clients or impact for the community they believe in. It is a powerful and demanding master, yet one that is willingly followed by most in the nonprofit sector. This master creates art, heals people, educates our youth, houses the homeless, and feeds the hungry. This master works for clean air, the preservation of wilderness, and it advocates for myriad diseases and other issues in our society.

But nonprofits must also serve the masters of their revenue and expense: stewarding their donors, fulfilling the requirements of grantors, government policies, third-party payers, buyers, and contractors. These many varied and multiple sources of revenue available to nonprofit organizations can make this master seem like a many-headed monster. As I have often heard my friend, Jon Pratt, executive director of the Minnesota Council of Nonprofits, remind nonprofit leaders, "If you take the king's shilling, you do the king's bidding." This master can have different requirements and sometimes feels juxtaposed against or contrary to the direction provided by the mission master.

Quite often, there are other masters as well. The community has major ownership in the nonprofit organization by right of preferential tax and economic treatment. Politicians, bureaucrats, policy makers, and auditors are other masters that expect homage at certain times and in certain ways.

Volunteers are sometimes masters who need care and feeding as well. The value they bring to your organization's ability to fulfill its mission can be minimal or all-encompassing depending on the quality and quantity of your volunteer contingent. We will spend more time discussing the relationship with volunteers in another chapter.

The presenting questions for investigation in this chapter are: Do you really know who your customers/clients/stakeholders/patrons are? How do you know what they want or need? Do the different groups that the organization serves require different services or products? Do they expect to be treated similarly or differently?

So let's investigate how your organization serves its clients, customers, patrons, donors, and stakeholders.

> Different organizations use different terminology to describe the people who receive benefit from the work they do. Arts organizations refer to patrons, counseling services to clients, health care calls them patients, retail services define them as customers, advocacy groups refer to them as constituents. Donors, members, participants, funders, and contributors are other terms to describe people with a special relationship to the organization. Frequently I will use the term client(s) or stakeholder(s) as an inclusive term to represent any or potentially all of these groups and subgroups.
>
> **definition**

Client/Customer Satisfaction

The following is a list of potential customer/client satisfaction, donor stewardship, and stakeholder engagement practices, processes, actions, and opportunities in a nonprofit organization. They are captured within the level/symbol where they most appropriately fit along a continuum of legal requirements to excellent practices. Determine your adherence to the practice or action with a check in the box.

🛑 STOP — Red–Stop (Legal Requirements)

✓	Practice or Action
	Donor and other stakeholder (especially client and patient) records are private and are not shared with any external agency or person except as prescribed by law.
	Legal requirements for reporting various conditions or situations (abuse or neglect for example) are clearly understood by all staff and volunteers, and actions on those requirements are undertaken as required by local or state mandates.
	Where required (or important), volunteers undergo background checks or legal validation with local or other authorities as appropriate.
	Nondiscriminatory policies and practices are in place and upheld by all staff and volunteers across our organization.

The only legal ramifications about satisfying your stakeholders are requirements around physical and emotional client protection, donor and stakeholder privacy, and protection of data. If you follow health and welfare reporting requirements, protect client information, and don't sell your donor lists, you probably have the legal concerns covered.

There are significant ethical responsibilities to understanding and responding to client satisfaction and dissatisfaction about your services. Working toward greater stakeholder satisfaction will benefit your organization in myriad fashion. Let's look at some of these from an ethical perspective.

⚠️ CAUTION — Yellow–Caution (Principled Ethics and Transparency)

✓	Practice or Action
	Our organization works with other similar organizations in our community to make sure there is no duplication of services being offered.
	Our organization works with other similar organizations in our community to make sure that all stakeholders' needs are being met.
	Fees and other charges are readily available and understood by our clients. Reasonable or alternative accommodations are made in the event someone cannot afford the stated cost of service.
	Various means are utilized to ensure that our clients from differing cultures or languages understand policies and procedures, fees, and other accommodations.
	Our organization does everything possible to make clients secure and comfortable during the process and provision of services.

✓	Practice or Action
	Communication with donors about their gifts, including receipts, thank-you letters, and clarification of restrictions, is completed in a timely manner.
	Quid quo pro (exchange of value) agreements or relationships with clients or stakeholders are strictly prohibited and enforced.

Solid ethical standards in dealing with clients and stakeholders promote the organizational transparency necessary for good community relations. Openness in those relationships promotes solid ethics. It is an appropriate circle. Getting close to the slippery slope of questionable relationships and transactions has caused many a good organization to cave once the issue sees the light of day.

Ethical and transparency issues are not just for leadership. The actions of frontline staff have caused some large organizations to stumble and fall. Ethical practices must be infused and expected throughout the organization.

It is also appropriate to consider the reasons for continuing to offer programs and services that may no longer be needed or effective. We might think we know what our customers and clients need based on what they said two or three years ago. But a lot has changed in that time. Our clients' needs might have changed as well.

GO Green–Go (Good Work/Growing Capacity)

✓	Practice or Action
	Program and other leaders demonstrate that the organization is open to new participants and welcomes new ideas.
	The organization has a process to communicate regularly with its stakeholders.
	The organization provides opportunities for the members of the community and its stakeholders to have input into the way or manner in which services are delivered.
	The organization uses several and varied means by with stakeholders can comment on their satisfaction or dissatisfaction with services or their delivery.
	The organization has a focused and effective process for quickly handling and solving client and stakeholder complaints and dissatisfaction.
	The organization has a process for collecting and storing stakeholder data, including demographic, relationship, and satisfaction data.
	Stakeholder data are regularly analyzed and managed in a way that is actionable and will improve the organization's products and services.

✓	Practice or Action
	The organization has a number of different ways that stakeholders can connect with it and get information about the services and programs that are offered.
	Input about program satisfaction or evaluation of program services is accomplished regularly and as proximate to the delivery of that service or product as possible.
	Program and executive leaders regularly and proactively gather input from stakeholders about their satisfaction with the services and the manner in which services are delivered.

> **Definition:** Process refers to a regular, repeatable, and often-documented activity that is undertaken to accomplish a task.

Growing organizations are starting to make changes based on what they learn from their clients. They are proactive about engaging clients in the development and modification of programs.

🏅 Blue Ribbon (Superior Quality)

✓	Practice or Action
	There is a process to formally identify and categorize different groups of people and individuals as constituents, clients, customers, patrons, patients, donors, or other stakeholders in terms of their relationship to the organization.
	Based on the size and scope of the organization, its stakeholder groups are subdivided into categories and segments based on internal criteria that help identify the breadth and depth or significance of the relationship to the organization.
	The organization uses several and varied means by which clients and stakeholders can comment on their satisfaction or dissatisfaction with services or their delivery.
	The organization has a focused and effective process for quickly handling and solving client and stakeholder complaints and dissatisfaction.
	The organization has a process for collecting and storing client and stakeholder data, including demographic, relationship, and satisfaction data.
	Client and stakeholder data are regularly analyzed and managed in a way that is actionable and will improve the organization's products and services.
	Staff understands what the customers/clients/stakeholders want and how best to deliver the product or service to meet those needs.
	There is a formal, systematic process in place to determine changes in the needs and wishes of clients over time.
	The organization communicates the information about client needs, wishes, and satisfaction with the board of directors, staff, volunteers, and other stakeholders.

Superior organizations are putting processes in place and improving those processes to look at clients and stakeholders as smaller subgroups and/or individuals and determine needs and wishes different from those of the whole client base. They take the input from their clients very seriously and act on that input.

Client satisfaction is moving to a deeper level. Questions are now more about "Will you recommend us to your friends?" and "Have you recommended us to your friends?" as well as about how satisfied the client was with the service or product.

Gold Cup (Preeminent Practice/Excellence)

✓	Practice or Action
	The organization has processes in place to build and strengthen relationships with its current stakeholders and the community as a means to discover and acquire new stakeholders, retain its current stakeholders, and deepen their relationship with the organization.
	The organization regularly makes changes to the method or process of delivery of the products or services based on information obtained from its clients and stakeholders. That new process is immediately scrutinized to determine the value of the improvement.
	The organization investigates what other similar programs or organizations are doing to meet the needs and expectations of their clients as a means of learning and improving.
	Donors are asked how they want to be recognized and thanked for their gifts.
	A variety of different means and methods are used by the organization to communicate with its clients and different groups of stakeholders encouraging two-way communications with those varied groups and individuals.
	The organization regularly and proactively gathers input from its clients and stakeholders about the effectiveness and efficiency (as different from satisfaction) of the delivery of their services and it has a process in place to use that information to innovate and improve its services.

A Gold Cup organization regularly improves and provides innovative services and turns clients into referents. Relationships with stakeholders are long term and positive. The Gold Cup organization is a positive-practices organization and provides management ideas for other organizations. Its long-term stakeholder relationships have probably resulted in significant financial reserves and perhaps an operational endowment.

Customers, donors, stakeholders, patients, patrons, students, participants—no matter what we call them—are the reason for our existence. All of them have ideas about how they want to be treated and the end result they want from working with your program or organization. We owe it to them, no matter who they are, to do our very best to meet their needs and wishes.

To Recap

- Listening to your clients and caring about their satisfaction is critical to providing quality services.

- Discovering what your clients really want and need and then acting on that information will make better use of scarce resources.

- There are many good and appropriate ways that can be used to find out about your clients/customers; surveys are just one.

- Organizational attitude and culture will determine the approach toward discovery of your client's satisfaction. Make sure you have an inquisitive nature.

Chapter Seven

Deadly Saying Four: "My Intuition Is Usually Right"

IN THIS CHAPTER

- Evaluation and measurement
- Questions about measurement
- Knowing what works and why
- Using meaningful data for program evaluation

Sometimes evaluation gets a bad rap because we fear it might indicate that we are doing something that is less than positive. It might tell us that what we are doing is actually counterproductive. In addition, change is hard for organizations and especially their human components to accept. But the limitations of funding, the demands of accreditation, the expectations of our clients and stakeholders make getting better a requirement, not an option. Getting better, all the time and in every way, is a critical and vital component of being a viable and valuable nonprofit. Getting better is the essence of evaluation.

Losing the Seniors

For several months now, the number of participants at the Senior Sneakers Exercise Program had been decreasing. Sure, there had been a number of changes to the program. The location had changed because of some remodeling in the usual setting. After all, it is hard to count on the availability of a church basement, the program director, Carol defended. Then, in the new site, the time had changed to accommodate another group, and the parking was not so convenient. But these kinds of changes happened all the time with other programs, Carol considered. After-school care and the eating healthy lunch program had also had to move for one reason or another. Both of them had transitioned with little slump in attendance.

And now there was that criticism about the program. The receptionist had relayed several messages of complaint to Carol. No names given, nothing specific. Several people just didn't like what was happening.

The CEO had heard too. She questioned Carol about it after the staff meeting. "What is happening?" she asked. "What is the problem?"

"It must be the new exercise leader," Carol opined. "He seemed to start out fine a year ago when I hired him. He must be goofing off or making them work too hard. I'll have a good talk with him in the morning. I'm sure that is the problem. After all, my intuition about these things is usually right."

Fix the Budget

The task force had been meeting for over two hours. Its job seemed actually quite simple: recommend a plan to balance the budget for the after-school youth services program.

Susan, the program director, had been given the responsibility to present a plan for a 20 percent increase of revenue, a similar reduction of cost, or a combination of the two in order to balance the budget the last half of the fiscal year.

Susan had enlisted two of her peers, Ray and Amy, directors in other areas, and one trusted program staff person, Hani. Last year Ray had needed to cut back and Amy had seen reductions in other areas as well. Hani had been in the program the longest of any of the staff and would soon be taking on program director responsibilities herself. They were a good group of people to work on this difficult and distasteful task. They trusted each other and would discuss the issue openly.

The program itself was rather disjointed and disheveled. There were somewhere between seven and thirteen youth workers and a couple of dozen volunteers on any given day to handle a group of about fifty to 125 third through seventh graders. Sports activities, homework, tutoring in math and reading, and after-school snacks were all part of the routine between three and seven o'clock each school night.

They had looked at the numbers of youth and the budget expenditures and debated significantly the merits of various components of the program. They compared what numbers they had against last year and projected expenses for the next six months.

When it came time to finalize the recommendation to the executive director, Susan spoke: "I know we've debated the merits of a couple of options for cutting expenses. None of them really look good. So I'm going to propose to the executive director that we reduce the hours our program operates by an hour each day. That gets us close to the 20 percent, and that way we won't have to cut any staff and everyone will just be paid a little less. I just think this is the best thing to do, and my intuition is usually right."

Complacent Staff

The number of people completing the jobs-training program was dropping, and the employers who depended on this labor force were frustrated. Jamal, the workforce development manager, had seen it coming. By his estimate, the skills level of the workers enrolling in the program was lower than it had been three years ago. They were just not getting the same caliber of participant.

Yet the employers were demanding trained workers, and there were no more financial or time resources available to the program. The county expected the program to place participants in a job within six weeks—no longer. Jamal's employment counselors had not had the opportunity to receive additional training themselves and were doing the same things they had for years.

Approaching his executive director, Aimee, Jamal inquired about support to appear before the county board of commissioners with a request for additional financial support or a relaxing of time requirements.

"I'm pretty sure they won't go for it," Aimee replied. "You don't have any information to suggest that the client base is harder to serve, and I haven't seen any differences. I've been watching your staff in action, though. I think they are just getting complacent. Better get after them. You know that my intuition about these things is usually right."

Questions about Measurement and Evaluation

- What data do you collect and review on a regular basis?

- What indicators of performance beyond financial measures are gathered, analyzed, and utilized on a regular basis to inform and improve organizational and program performance? Who reviews these data?

- How are data compared and with what?

- Are level, trend, and comparative data available for use by leadership and management?

- How are data used in decision making?

- Are the data you collect and review important to the organization, and are they integrated to appropriate levels of management in the organization?

- Are the data understood in the same way by everyone who reviews them?

- Are any of the data you collect "leading" (future-looking) data, or are they all "lagging" (past) data?

- How is staff involved in the collection, review, analysis, and utilization of data to improve? How is the board involved?

> **observation**
>
> In the absence of measurement, management will assume the problem is people... and people will assume the problem is management!

- What data are shared outside the organization to validate performance? How are they shared?

- How are data stored and secured inside the organization? How do you manage your data collection, storage and dissemination processes, technology, and security?

- Are your private and confidential data stored and secured in such a way that they are truly private and confidential?

We frequently use our intuition, perceptions, and experiences to make decisions. Our survival seems to depend on reacting quickly to adverse conditions. Operating a program or an organization in this fashion will ultimately lead to disaster.

Operating by the Numbers

Practice does *not* make perfect. You can continue to practice bad habits and stay the same or even get worse. Only *perfect* practice makes perfect. But perfection for most of us is a long way off. So how about making progress? How about just getting better?

That is what evaluation is about. Getting better. Getting better at serving our clients. Getting better at stewarding our resources. Getting better at changing people's lives. Getting better at making a positive impact in the community.

Intuition seldom, if ever, helps us do that. We need to see, hear, smell, touch, or taste improvement. And if we can grasp it with our senses, then we can measure it, and it can give us information to use to improve what we do. So if we can see, hear, smell, touch, or taste something, intuition is found wanting. Evaluation is the answer.

Evaluation carries the innuendo of change in order to fix something that is broken or that we have not done a good job of *doing* our jobs. And it should, for that is one of the potential products of evaluation. Summative evaluation looks at the end result of a program or activity to determine results.

But it is not the only use. Formative valuation can help us get better at doing important work. It can help us improve activities that are already good. It will help our processes improve and become more efficient.

Evaluation does promote change. And change is hard for organizations and especially their human components to accept. We don't like changing the things we have gotten comfortable doing.

> *Are you any good? Are you getting better? How do you know?*
>
> —Mark Blazey, National Baldrige Award Evaluator and Trainer

Evaluation and measurement are part of life. A critical, important part of life. At birth, a baby is given an APGAR assessment score… evaluation. In school, a student takes a test and gets a report card… evaluation. We go to our medical provider for a checkup or concern… evaluation. And our blood pressure and pulse are taken… evaluation. We take the car in to the mechanic because of a curious noise and the blinking dashboard light… evaluation. Appliances and products get three, four, or five stars… evaluation. We keep score during a golf game… evaluation. Baseball pitchers are known for their earned run averages… evaluation. Sellers are rated on eBay… evaluation. And on, and on, and on…

Knowing What Works and Why

In order to evaluate, you need to understand why and how your activities are designed to help people change their lives. Your program or organization must be able to articulate a theory of change and a logical or causal model showing the relationship between the resources you use, your activities, the outputs of the program, and the outcomes you want and expect to produce.

If you are unfamiliar with logic model, theory of change, program map, or other methods of articulating your program theory, you most certainly will want to investigate some of the many great resources that can assist you and your organization in identifying this chain of events. A good introductory *Logic Model Development Guide* can be found on the website of the W.K. Kellogg Foundation. The University of Wisconsin-Extension website is another source. Even Wikipedia offers some help. Many of the concepts, terms, measures, and indicators described in this chapter are more comprehensible with a solid working knowledge of program theory.

> *There is nothing so practical as a good theory.*
>
> –Kurt Lewin (1890–1947), Pioneer of Social and Organizational Psychology

After we accept that evaluation is important and understand the theory of change our program encourages, we need data to use in that evaluation. Our intuition, as good as it might be, does not provide us with usable data.

The limitations of funding, the demands of accreditation, the expectations of our clients and stakeholders make getting better a requirement, not an option. In order to get better at what we do, we need data. We need to turn data into information, and we need to use that information in leading and managing our nonprofit organizations.

What kind of data should we capture? How many measures are appropriate? How frequently should we look at data? These are all questions needing answers.

The following is a list of potential evaluation, measurement, and data management practices, processes, actions, and opportunities of a nonprofit organization. They are captured within the level/symbol where they most appropriately fit along a continuum of legal requirements to excellent practices. Determine your adherence to the practice or action with a check in the box.

🛑 STOP Red–Stop (Legal Requirements)

✓	Practice or Action
	All client, donor, and stakeholder data are kept confidential and not shared outside the organization unless permission to do so is previously provided by the stakeholder.
	A process is in place that allows a donor or stakeholder to remain anonymous.
	A process is in place that allows a donor or stakeholder to be removed from organizational mailing lists or excluded from receiving future (phone, mail, and email) communications from the organization.

> *One accurate measurement is worth more than a thousand expert opinions.*
>
> –Admiral Grace Hooper (1906–1992), US Navy Rear Admiral and Computer Scientist

Aside from compiling the requisite data to file your Form 990, there is little legal requirement for data gathering, dissemination, or evaluation.

There are, however, some requirements for keeping your data secure and out of the hands of people who do not need them or might use them inappropriately.

⚠️ CAUTION Yellow–Caution (Principled Ethics and Transparency)

✓	Practice or Action
	A financial budget is established for each fiscal year. It realistically anticipates revenue and expense for that time period.
	Total revenues and total expenses to date are captured and regularly reviewed at each board meeting.
	Revenues and expenses are regularly reviewed at each board meeting against budgeted amounts.
	A balance of accounts (balance sheet) is produced regularly for review at each of our board meetings.
	On at least an annual basis, our organization provides objective data to the community about our program and organizational activities and accomplishments.
	Our client data are collected, stored, and secured in a way that inhibits them from being inadvertently viewed or shared outside the organization.
	Our organization has a confidentiality policy that indicates it will not share, sell, or trade stakeholder data with other organizations.
	Our board of directors, staff, and volunteers sign a confidentiality agreement that indicates their agreement to abide by organizational confidentiality policies.

The Yellow-Caution category is about ethics and meeting the minimum standards of watchdog agencies that establish and publish benchmarks for donor information and data security. It may be that you are a small or new organization or perhaps do not track some of the financial ratios and other data necessary to present your organization for consideration by these groups. If so, these expectations can be used as objectives to be attained.

Ethically, even a small organization, one not required to have a formal audit or submit a 990, will want to provide as much information about its activities, outputs, and outcomes as it possibly can provide to the community that supports it.

Having and understanding basic financial data and adherence to privacy and data security issues are primary considerations for fundraising and effective organizational management. Questions in the Yellow-Caution category will challenge your organization to ensure that it is living by acceptable standards of data management.

GO Green–Go (Good Work/Growing Capacity)

✓	Practice or Action
	Data are captured from many of our organization's programs.
	Data are collected in a way that appreciates and considers the cultural norms, practices, and expectations of the person or group being evaluated.
	Data are regularly and consistently used in decision making.
	All measurement and financial data are securely backed up for preservation on a routine basis.
	Data are reviewed regularly by the people in the organization who are best equipped to do something about what the data are indicating.
	Standards for external accreditation and approval of practice by outside assessors are being incorporated into the management practice with the anticipation of meeting or exceeding standards.
	Data on the achievement of positive changes in people's lives (outcomes) are gathered.
	Management and fundraising expense as a percentage of all expense is calculated at least annually.
	Program expense as a percentage of overall revenue is calculated at least annually.
	The cost to raise a dollar is calculated for specific fundraising endeavors as well as the overall fundraising program.
	The cost/benefit ratio or return on investment of programs on an individual stakeholder or group basis is calculated regularly.

Green-Go category is about starting to really use data to get better. The ethical considerations of collecting and storing data have been ensured and there is an attitude among the organization's leadership that it wants to use data to get better.

But more than a simple desire to use measurement for management decisions is necessary. First there must be collection of data. Then the data need to be turned into information. And, finally, they can be analyzed to improve practice.

Blue Ribbon (Superior Quality)

✓	Practice or Action
	The anticipated uses of the data are explored and determined before the data are collected.
	Data are collected from all facets of the organization, including support function areas such as human resources and information technology.
	Measures are reviewed by program management on a routine and regular basis, and management or operational action is taken on the basis of the data.
	Data are trend-lined and compared against past accomplishments as well as against future goals and expectations.
	External validation, accreditation, or assessments are routinely undertaken as part of the process of meeting standards and learning in the organization.
	Important measures are reviewed by governance and executive leadership on a regular basis and organizational or strategic action is taken on the basis of the data.
	There is a process in place to gather appropriate data to analyze the health of the whole organization beyond financial statements.
	Backup of data is routine, secure, and redundant.

Superior measurement and evaluation includes looking at programmatic improvement, change, and growth, as well as organizational factors for improvement and relationships among programs. All programming is impacted by the health and well-being of the parent organization. To that end, some whole organizational assessment is happening.

Use of data to drive decision making is understood and accepted as part of the culture of the organization. Governance has the correct information for strategic and policy decisions, and leadership and management both make use of data to drive organizational performance.

Mainline staff and volunteers also understand the need for data and collect them regularly, willingly, and accurately. Data are current and valid.

Gold Cup (Preeminent Practice/Excellence)

✓	Practice or Action
	Trends in programmatic outputs and outcomes are tracked on the smallest time increment reasonable for our organization.
	Our organization works to track its impact on the community based on its programming.
	Our organization works collaboratively with other organizations, providing data and information to assist in determining community impact as a result of the work of multiple organizations and programs.
	The organization has developed a culture that uses data at every step for decision making and dedication of resources.
	Client and staff satisfaction are very high as a result of consistent evaluation and improvement.
	There is an expectation of regular and constant improvement of programmatic and administrative processes.
	Stretch goals for accomplishment of mission activities are routinely set and frequently met.
	Data used throughout the organization are deemed important to leadership and management of the programs and organization.
	Evaluation of the process of data collection is accomplished on an ongoing basis, ensuring the integrity of the data and the collection process.
	Aggregated and anonymous data are shared and compared with similar organizations in order to improve outcomes for our clientele and impact for the community.
	The importance of specific data collection and use is integrated throughout the organization. Everybody understands why it is collected and how it is used.

At the highest level of evaluation and measurement, the process of evaluation and data collection itself is being evaluated, modified, and tweaked to provide better information. Analyses of data are happening more frequently and with greater detail. Staff and volunteers at all levels of the organization understand and contribute to the collection and analysis of the data for which they are responsible.

Measurement and evaluation at this point have embedded themselves to the culture, and decisions, both small and large, are data driven. Decisions are seldom, if ever, made without the use of accurate, current data. There is a true culture of learning and desire to get better. High levels or exemplary scores are attained on accreditation or external validation assessments.

> **observation**
> One of the first things that flying students learn is to rely on their instruments and not their intuition for accurate information. Many lives have been lost because of a failure to believe the instrumentation.

Intuition is almost always found wanting in the face of meaningful data. Still, many nonprofit leaders continue to scoff at the idea of measurement or ignore the data that are in front of them. Others are inundated with measures that mean little but need to be reported nonetheless. Somebody thinks they need them for something.

Accurate, timely, important, and actionable data are critical to effective leadership and management.

To Recap

- ◆ Collecting and using meaningful data for program evaluation is a critical component of providing quality services.

- ◆ Using evaluation for improved program effectiveness and efficiency will positively impact your organizational financial position.

- ◆ The main reason for improving effectiveness and efficiency should be to serve your clients better.

Chapter Eight

Deadly Saying Five: "Our Staff and Volunteers Are Simply the Best!"

IN THIS CHAPTER

- Valuing our people... our wonderful human resources
- Questions about your human resource management
- Managing our valuable human resources
- Organizational culture and climate

Every nonprofit organization has good, caring people working and volunteering to accomplish its mission. Providing for them and managing their efforts on behalf of the organization's mission is what makes the difference between good and great services in your organization.

One More Sacrifice

"I know it is a lot to ask," Audrey began. "And I promise it won't happen again."

"Sure," Jim said under his breath to Hassam and Domingo. "That is what she told us last year when she said there would be no salary increases. Now we have to take a 5 percent pay cut. What's next, our health benefits?"

Audrey was the board treasurer, asking staff for some more slack so that the organization would be able to pay its operating loan and regain its line of credit.

Jim continued: "This is just another sacrifice that we have been asked to make over the past two years."

"I know," Domingo enjoined. "First it was the mileage reimbursement that went. Then a freeze on hires, leaving everyone working fifty-plus hours per week."

"It's not like we make a lot," Hassam stated. "With a master of social work degree, I could do a lot better at the hospital or the county, but I like what we do. Working with new immigrant families is really important to me. I'm not in it to get rich, but it would be nice to be able to live above the poverty line and actually have health and retirement benefits."

Closing the meeting, Audrey smiled and turned to the executive director. "Our staff is simply the best," she concluded.

Fishing Buddies

"What? Tough day?" Janice asked Tammy as she walked into the restroom and noticed her almost in tears.

"Yeah, and I don't know what to do?"

"What's up?" asked Janice.

"It's that volunteer, Norman," Tammy stated. "This is now the fourth time he's tried to corner me back in the storage room. He's been bumping up against me and reaching around me every chance he gets. He just won't stop! I've tried to tell him politely to not get so close, and I've been trying to avoid working next to him, but it is pretty hard. You know how busy we've been around here."

"That I do know," Janice stated. "It's hard to even find time to go to the bathroom! So, have you mentioned this to anyone else?"

"Yeah. I told Fred, the director, a couple of weeks ago, and he said it must be all in my head. He said that Norm is a great guy and that Norm not only volunteers a couple of days a week, but he's a super donor too. The annual report shows that he gives us a couple thousand a year. Fred said that he figured it was just my imagination and lack of work experience. None of the older staff have ever said anything about Norm."

"So, Fred thinks that just because you are young and good looking you should have to put up with this?" Janice asked.

"Apparently," Tammy responded. "It was even worse yesterday when, after giving Norm the Volunteer of the Quarter plaque, Fred looked at me and winked when he patted Norm on the back and said that our volunteers are simply the best."

"Isn't there someone you can talk to?" Janice queried and then responded, "You shouldn't have to put up with that."

"I don't know. The executive director really likes both Norm and Fred. They go fishing together sometimes. I guess I'll have to live with it," Tammy acknowledged softly as the tears really did begin to fall.

A Black Hole

"Well," bemoaned Crystal. "Just like last time."

"What?" asked Vito. "What's happened?"

"So," Crystal continued, "I went to Ricardo with this brochure about a leadership seminar next month, hoping to attend. It looks like a couple of the speakers have some program ideas we really could use. One of them has been doing similar work for ten years and has a doctoral degree in the field. It really seems like our program could use some of the information. And there are some other sessions on leadership and management practices."

"Yeah. By the looks of the program, I'd agree. I'd like to go too. What did Ricardo say?"

"Same as usual, Vito. He said there wasn't any money in the budget for program staff to attend any seminars or conferences. He said he'd go and bring the information back to us. He said we do such a great job with the clients that we probably wouldn't learn much anyway. He said that we're simply the best."

"So, as usual," Vito replied, "the info will end up in the black hole of the executive director's office. Ricardo's idea of doing a great job is simply doing what he says. I wonder if we'll ever get to learn how to get better?"

Questions about Our Human Resources: Staff and Volunteers

- ◆ Does your organization comply with all the applicable laws and regulations relative to employment and volunteer engagement? How do you ascertain compliance? How is it audited?

- ◆ Are your board and workforce diverse, and do they represent the community and the clients/customers/stakeholders with whom you work?

- ◆ How do you know what your staff and volunteers need and appreciate? How do you engage them and reward them for their efforts?

- ◆ How do you develop your staff and volunteers and better equip them for the work they do?

- ◆ Is the climate and culture of your organization supportive of the personal needs and professional interests of your staff and volunteers?

- ◆ Do you have processes and policies in place for succession, communication of grievances, conflicts of interest, safety, evaluation of performance, compensation, etc.?

Valuing Our People, Our Wonderful Human Resource

Known to be a bit sarcastic on occasion, I might ask: "What are your staff and volunteers the best at? Working long hours with little pay and doing good things with few resources?" Because that is what we expect of our peers in the sector, right? I've heard it a myriad of times: "I'm not in the nonprofit sector to get rich." Yes, but it would be nice to be able to live above the poverty line and actually have health and retirement benefits.

So, what duty, care, and loyalty do you have for the people who are the life force of this nonprofit organization of yours? They need to be supported. They need care and feeding as much as your funders do, yet we often take them for granted.

While it is expected that nonprofit staff, volunteers, and other stakeholders have more than a passing interest in the mission of your organization, it is unusual that they will bring with them all of the skills and knowledge required for excellent performance. Leadership needs to supply them with the resources, including training and information, to accomplish their expected tasks. Engaging the staff and volunteers, keeping them satisfied with their work, supplying them with appropriate compensation and reward, developing and enhancing their skills and competency, and evaluating their effectiveness against a set of predetermined objectives are all components of this focus on the stewardship of your human resources.

Do you identify the resources and training your staff and volunteers need to do their jobs and demonstrate appreciation for it? How do you engage them and reward them for their efforts? How do you develop your staff members and better equip them for the work they do now or might do in the future? Are there ways we encourage staff to explore and grow outside the programmatic area of responsibility?

The climate and culture of your organization must be supportive of the needs and interests of your staff and volunteers as well as the clientele. The workforce should be as diverse as the community and the clients/customers/stakeholders with whom you work.

Do you have processes and policies for succession, communication of grievances, conflicts of interest, worker safety, evaluation of performance, compensation, etc.?

The following is a list of potential staff, volunteers, human resource management practices, processes, actions, and opportunities in a nonprofit organization. They are captured within the level/color where they most appropriately fit along a continuum of legal requirements to excellent practices. Determine your adherence to the practice or action with a check in the box.

STOP Red–Stop (Legal Requirements)

✓	Practice or Action
	Key leaders with human resources responsibilities understand and apply the legal requirements of federal, state, and local government as they apply to hiring and employment practices.

Deadly Saying Five: "Our Staff and Volunteers Are Simply the Best!"

✓	Practice or Action
	Withholding and payment of FICA and other payroll taxes are done faithfully and immediately when payroll is distributed to employees.
	Loans or related financial transactions are not taken from or provided to employees or volunteers, including members of the board of directors.
	Background checks are conducted for all staff and volunteers where required by state of local ordinance. Background investigations or bonding may also be deemed appropriate because of the nature of their work with specific groups of people or when handling finances or confidential data.
	The workplace meets ADA requirements and is physically accessible to most people.
	Work safety and OSHA regulations are applied and enforced for the benefit of our staff, volunteers, and clients.

Paying attention to these issues can save your organization a lawsuit or prevent an injury. Not paying attention to or ignorance of these issues could result in fines, organizational closure, or worse. Ignorance is not bliss in these areas. Ignorance is just ignorance.

CAUTION | Yellow–Caution (Principled Ethics and Transparency)

✓	Practice or Action
	Your organization has a written conflict-of-interest policy that prohibits members of the board of directors and employees from engaging in any conflicting or interested party transactions and requires disclosure of relationships, nepotism, and other potential conflicts of interest.
	There is a formal policy and process in place that allows for the confidential reporting and investigation of any potential or real illegal activities within your organization (whistle-blower policy). This policy is known, understood, and consistently enforced.
	Policies and practices to uphold data privacy regulations relative to employee information and documents are in place and consistently applied.
	There is both policy and a cultural understanding among staff and volunteers that lying, cheating, stealing, or other illegal or unethical acts are not acceptable behaviors.
	Staff might have been, or it is expected that they would be, reprimanded or terminated for inappropriate behavior.
	Staff and volunteers are polite and generally caring with each other and the clients.
	Even when not required, accommodations for employees or volunteers with special abilities or disabilities are accomplished as reasonably possible.

Often, breaches of ethics in a nonprofit organization are as serious for the mission of the organization as an illegal activity. The public often does not distinguish between the appearance of wrongdoing and actual wrongdoing.

But organizations of our sector have even a stronger obligation to be ethical and transparent. We carry a public trust that resonates across the sector. If unethical behaviors are discovered in one organization, others suffer by association. We owe it to our clients and our partners in mission to behave well and ethically.

GO Green–Go (Good Work/Growing Capacity)

✓	Practice or Action
	Board-approved personnel policies are appropriate to the size and diversity of your staff. The policies are regularly updated and available to and understood by all employees.
	Equity and fair play are evident in all human relations and staff policies, benefits, and practices.
	Our organization is beginning to consider the importance of satisfied and engaged workers. An assessment of staff and volunteer morale and satisfaction has been done.
	All new employees are trained to accomplish the job for which they are hired. Ongoing and augmented training is regularly provided for all staff to help them improve products or service delivery.
	All new employees receive a review of their initial performance and recommendations and assistance toward improvement.
	All employees and volunteers have written descriptions of their job positions and the expectations for performance of those jobs.
	All employees receive formal, written reviews of their job performance at least annually, preferably more frequently.
	All regular volunteers receive reviews of their performance on a regular basis that is tied to the significance of the work they do.
	Our board of directors regularly reviews and approves the overall compensation schedule and benefits package for employees, striving for fair and equitable market-based reimbursement.
	Our board of directors regularly reviews the performance of the executive director against a set of predetermined goals or expectations.
	Our board of directors establishes and reviews the salary of the executive director, striving for a fair and market-based reimbursement salary and benefits package.
	Our organization offers and encourages the ongoing education and training of its employees to enhance both their personal growth and the capability of the organization.

✓	Practice or Action
	To the extent possible, our nonprofit provides financial resources and time for employees to access education and training.
	Our organization makes a concerted effort to employ staff and engage volunteers who represent the diversity of the community we serve.
	Accommodations are made for family responsibilities as much as possible given the job requirements of the staff person.
	The psychological environment and culture of our organization's workplace is safe and healthy.

Green and growing organizations of the nonprofit sector care as much for their staff and human resources as they do for their clients and customers. It also makes good financial sense to treat your employees well and your volunteers caringly. Some estimate the cost to replace an employee at one and one-half times that person's annual salary. And that doesn't even take into account the team building and other aspects of reorganization that are required when the new employee arrives.

Blue Ribbon (Superior Quality)

✓	Practice or Action
	The temperature of staff morale and satisfaction is regularly taken and compared against national or local information.
	Programs have been initiated to increase staff morale, satisfaction, and recognition of exceptional job performance.
	All members of the staff and volunteers understand how their work contributes to fulfilling the mission and accomplishment of the strategic and operational plans.
	The organization allows for and encourages alternate holiday time off, accommodating the diversity of religious and ethnic practices among its staff and volunteers.
	Human resources policies and practices promote the hiring and retention of qualified employees.
	Regular continuing education and training in the area of staff's responsibility is expected, and financial and time assistance for that training is provided.
	Consideration is given to the succession of leaders and other key staff in the organization in order that services to stakeholders and the continuity of the organization are not unduly interrupted.
	Both staff and volunteers maintain the highest level of ethical behavior and uphold the values of the organization at all times. Regular discussion and training about ethical issues is accomplished.

Blue organizations take the care and feeding of their staff members very seriously. They tend to treat their volunteers similarly to paid staff and consider both staff and volunteers to be the critical link to mission accomplishment and top notch performance. There are few if any surprises for or about employees and the relationships between all staff and administration are caring and professional. It is obvious to a visitor or a collaborative partner that the staff works well together and cares about each other as teammates.

Gold Cup (Preeminent Practice/Excellence)

✓	Practice or Action
	The climate of the organization is conducive to healthy life and family relationships, allowing a positive work/life balance and providing adequate vacation and personal time away from job responsibilities.
	The structure, practices, and policies of the organization promote and encourage direct and open communication among all staff and stakeholders throughout and at all levels within the organization.
	Staff leadership and management growth and succession plans for key staff are in place, with several people in the organization capable of rising to more responsible positions should the need arise.
	Plans are in place and staff has the capacity and authority to carry out the mission of the organization in the absence of key management or organizational leadership.
	The organization is viewed as a training ground for nonprofit staff and leaders in its field of expertise.
	The climate of the workplace and formal policies are considerate of a diversity of peoples, including cultural, ethnic, religious backgrounds, and expectations.
	Contractors of the organization are obligated to uphold the same standards of ethics, values, and behavior as all other staff and volunteers.
	Compensation and other rewards and incentives are linked to accomplishment of goals and objectives or other performance-based criteria.
	Staff satisfaction and morale is exceptional. Vacant staff positions garner a significant number of qualified applicants and fill quickly.

The Gold Cup organization enjoys the benefits of a staff that is top notch and also contributes back to the community in many ways. Because of the breadth and depth of the staff team, the organization continues to perform at an exceptionally high level even in the absence of key leaders.

Supporting, caring, and encouraging the best of our people, our human resources, means more than developing and adopting a set of HR policies and procedures, although that in itself is a positive step forward. Solid nonprofit organizations look for people who share their vision and then value and nurture those staff and volunteers. They encourage their growth and applaud exceptional performance.

> Very few people show up for work planning to do a poor job. Often a poorly constructed process or a flawed system foils their attempts at doing good work and people get blamed. Changing people won't work if a broken system or process is the problem.
>
> **observation**

To Recap

- ◆ Valuing and managing your staff and volunteers, that wonderful human resource you have, is vital to the work of your organization.

- ◆ Another critical factor is your organizational culture and climate. What is it like and does it enhance or detract from your work?

- ◆ Because your organization benefits from staff who are healthy, knowledgeable, and always learning, it is important to invest in them.

Chapter Nine

Deadly Saying Six: "We've Never Done It That Way Before"

IN THIS CHAPTER

- Improving our work and fundraising processes
- Questions about process improvement
- Understanding your work and key processes
- Measuring how you do your work
- Working smart—managing and improving the way you work

In today's world, just staying the same is not an option. Because, guess what is happening all around you? Others are getting better. Staying the same means you are happy with the speed of a 386 computer processor or an MS DOS-based operating system, or with carrying a cell phone, camera, palm pilot, Tetris game, pager, and GPS as separate units. Staying the same means you are content getting your merchandise shipment in ten days to two weeks or scheduling your vehicle for oil change a week in advance.

Luddites at Work

"Thanks for coming," Jean stated, opening the meeting about camp registration. "I wanted to start this conversation early in the year so the same situation would not happen again."

"You mean about the loss of the registration cards, right?" questioned Alex, the waterfront director.

"Exactly right!" Jean proclaimed. "We cannot have a scene like last year. We had angry parents and kids running all over the place while we tried to figure out who paid and who did not, who

had their health check and who still needed to see the nurse, who signed up for which bunkhouse, and who had allergies. I'll resign as camp director before we do that again."

"So," Jean continued, "how are we going to be sure that the registration cards get packed in the van and not left in the front hall of the office? I was thinking that we should have someone responsible for making copies of the registration cards and putting them in two places. That way, if we lose one set, we'll have another to fall back on."

"What about going to an online registration?" Alex asked. "That way we would have the copies electronically and could get them up at camp even if we forgot the laptop or the hard copies. The main house has a satellite connection; I've seen it."

"Good idea," Samantha, the cook, injected. "I could even sort by field and see who needs a special diet without having to try to read the lousy handwriting of some of our parents. That would work great. I even know a software program we could use. I used it at another camp and it worked swell. The nurse and I were both able to see the kids' health info and make sure to keep the peanuts away from some of them."

"Now, just a minute." Jean cautioned. "We've been using the same registration forms for over ten years and most of the parents are comfortable filling them out. Some of them don't have computers, and what would happen if a computer crashed and we couldn't get the information out? It would be just like last year. I don't like this idea. We've never done it that way before."

Sorting the Mail

As the newly appointed interim executive director, I was making the rounds of offices to meet a couple of the staff I had not met the week before. The advertising sales manager's office was open, and I walked in to greet him. The Minnesota Twins jersey on the wall gave the opportunity to commiserate about yet another losing season. As I was preparing to leave, I noticed the check lying on one of the piles of papers on his desk. Well aware of the desperate situation of our cash flow, that several thousand dollars was a welcome sight.

"Hey! A check… great! When did we get this?" I asked, pointing to the cream-colored document and thinking it probably arrived yesterday.

"Oh," Gus said, "It came in the week before last. I haven't had time to write the sponsor a thank-you note. I should be able to get it in the bank this week."

"Thanks," I said, restraining myself. "That would be good. Try to get it done today, okay?"

With the new realization that there might be a problem or two left over from the former and founding executive of thirty-plus years, recently retired, I proceeded to query the receptionist. She was a likable lady, with a nice smile, and she made a good first impression for our visitors.

"Good, morning, Nancy," I sang. "I've got a question for you. What happens to the mail when the postal carrier delivers it?"

"Well," she started cautiously, not sure if she was in trouble and should cover her tracks or if she should be truthful. "I sort it all by staff member or department and I put it in their mailboxes. I keep the advertising and flyers in a box here (pointing under her desk), but everything else goes to the person it is addressed to."

"What do you do with checks?" I prodded, guessing that she was being truthful at this point.

"If I know there is a membership check in the envelope, I give it to the bookkeeper."

"Do you ever open any of the mail to see what is in it?"

"No, they don't want me to do that."

"Who are they?"

"The sales staff, the development director, and the events coordinator. They all said they don't want me to open any of the mail that is addressed to them."

By now, a couple of other staff members had overheard our conversation and were gathering, uncertain if they should be staying or not.

"Well, as of right now, you are opening all the mail." I declared rather firmly. "Yes, all the mail, unless it is marked 'Personal and Confidential' or something similar to that. I want you to take any checks that are in the mail and stamp them for deposit right away. Fill out a deposit slip and give the checks to the director of administration. She can then take them to the bank later in the day."

"But," Nancy wondered, flustered and knowing she was caught in the middle, "what if a staff member needs to see the check? They say they need to see it to enter the data correctly."

"Then you can give them a photocopy," I said, "but not the original. That goes to the bank immediately."

"All right," she agreed, "but I think there are going to be problems. We've just never done it that way before!"

I Don't Like the Changes

Returning from six weeks of family leave, Fernando found that there were some changes to the intake process, and he was not happy.

"What gives?" he complained to Gina, the intake supervisor. "I go away for a couple of weeks, and you change everything around. All of the forms are different, and I don't even get to talk to the new participants until after they fill out the forms. What is this all about?"

"We did some investigating," Gina explained. "We interviewed a number of clients and surveyed them for a month while you were away. The changes are a result of what we learned by analyzing *the surveys and interviews. A high percentage of clients felt it would be more helpful to meet with the intake worker after they had worked through the questions themselves. That way they would be able to ask better questions and the process would take less time. So far, our testing of this change has proved their ideas to be accurate."*

"I don't like it! My opinions and ideas have been providing good info on the best way to operate this intake process for years. I don't think a few surveys give better evidence than my years of experience," said Fernando.

"Well, for the time being at least, until we can survey our clients again, we're going to continue this way," explained Gina.

"You'll see, emphasized Fernando. "They'll want to go back the other way... the way it's been done for years. I just know it!"

Thanking the Donor... Quickly!

One large, nonprofit organization with which I was acquainted received many small contributions on a regular basis. Two staff members had primary responsibility for receiving, processing, and receipting those gifts, including sending thank-you notes to donors along with receipts. It was a relatively simple data-entry process, yet depending on the time of year, it was taking between three and fifteen business days to get the receipt and thank-you in the mail. As fundraisers know, it is important to acknowledge donations quickly while the thought of the gift is still fresh in the donor's mind.

Supervisory and managerial staff provided significant rationale for the time it was taking. The two staff members were dedicated, longtime employees and worked hard, sometimes overtime, to accomplish their work. But our donors deserved better. There needed to be a faster, more efficient way.

Over a period of several months, we methodically and meticulously tracked and wrote out each small step in the process from the time the gift came in the door, physically or electronically, to the time the thank-you card and receipt were in the mail. We created a map along two walls of a conference room showing each step in the process and identifying the time each step took.

The question: "Why are you doing it that way?" was asked repeatedly. Many times the spoken or unspoken response was "because that is the way we've always done it." Investigation revealed that five or six people from different areas in the organization were involved, several of whom were checking, rechecking, and rechecking once more the work accomplished by others earlier in the process.

Without losing any data integrity, we managed to move the time of the thanking and receipting process down to between twenty-four and seventy-two hours and eliminated one of the full-time positions in the deal, allowing that person to be shifted to another, more critical, part of the organization. The savings to the organization amounted to tens of thousands of dollars annually and offered a more positive donor stewardship message.

Questions about Working Smart and Improving Our Processes

The following questions raise some of the challenges of living and working in an environment that does not stand still for very long.

- How do you know that your activities, programs, and services are operating as effectively and efficiently as possible with the best possible outputs and outcomes?

- What measurement processes and measures do you use to determine efficiency and effectiveness?

- How are your programs developed and revised to meet new and changing client/customer/stakeholder needs?

- What innovations in program design or delivery have been made recently?

- How do you regulate and control the delivery of programs for consistency and effectiveness when delivered by different staff/volunteers or in different locations?

- How frequently do you review the process of delivery of programs for effectiveness?

Working Smart: Improving Our Work and Fundraising Processes

As humans, we can be complacent, we rather like being in a rut. We don't want to change unless there is a good reason and we know that the results will be better. We don't like that white-knuckle tension that goes with getting out of a rut.

But without the ability to change, we will never get better, we will never grow. And in order to get better and grow, we need to know exactly what we are doing and how well we are doing it. We need some information. We need to know how we are doing what we do and describe the process by which our product is made or our service delivered.

> Driving in North Country winters is a special skill and challenge. After a snowfall and before the roads get plowed, the first vehicle down the road creates a path—a rut—in the snow. It is easiest driving, as one of the following vehicles, to stay in that rut. Getting out of it, however, has its own excitement and difficulties. The wheels get thrown around, there is usually some slipping and sliding, the moment is tense... white-knuckle tense. Once out of the rut, however, the driving is again fairly smooth. It is the breaking free from the old way that is challenging.
>
> **observation**

Staying the same and accomplishing your work at the same speed or with the same quality as you did a year or three ago is no longer acceptable. You will lose ground significantly if that is your goal. Even keeping pace with others means improving, speeding, or refining our processes and performance. Being a nonprofit organization does not exempt us from the need to improve. If anything, we should have greater expectations about improvement than our business counterparts. After all, isn't what we do about changing lives, not just making money?

Change is both the constant and the nemesis of an organization. Without continual change and improvement, the rest of the world walks right on by and we fade into yesterday. Knowing the best direction of change and leading others along the path is a challenging proposition. You need to be innovative and improve performance, even while the status quo seems to be working.

Leadership is the critical and driving force behind process improvement. Without the impetus of leadership, there will be only limited change and most likely reactive change as a result of broken processes. Putting fires out is the lowest level of leadership. Good leaders look at things that are working well and ask about getting better. They want to "work smarter," not just harder.

Understanding Your Work and Key Processes

Before investigating these "working smart" issues, it is critical to identify the processes in our organizations. That means we need to stop and think about how we go about our everyday work. We need to identify our activities and the pieces that go into our programs as a series of individual steps or a process.

Some processes in your organization will be considered "key" or "critical" for the work you do. Without that process, you would not be able to accomplish your mission. And you must do it. A key process cannot be done by another organization on your behalf.

> *If you can't describe what you're doing as a process, you don't know what you're doing.*
>
> —W. Edwards Deming (1900–1993), Statistician and Business Strategist

One critical and key work process for many human service organizations is often called "intake." This is a very important process that begins the relationship with the client and is necessary in gathering the client's information. Most likely, it leads into another helping process for the client that is provided by the organization.

A theater might consider its reservations and ticketing, or "front office," process a critical function of its work of connecting the art with the patron. Having a staff member or volunteer visit with someone at home to accomplish a task or provide a service is another process, or perhaps several processes, of a program.

A food shelf or food pantry must have a process for acquiring food and donated commodities. It must have a process for intake of its clients. The food shelf will need a process for distribution of food to the client. Each of these processes is "key" and important to accomplishing the mission of the food shelf.

It will also need a process for cleaning the storage space. However, the cleaning process, as important as it is, does not attain the level of consideration as a "key" process for the food shelf. A custodial service or other agency could provide the staff to clean the space. It is not critical that it be done by the food shelf organization in order to fulfill its mission.

Defining each critical or "key" process in your organization is the first step to making that process work better.

Measuring How You Do Your Work

Each of these processes has a beginning and an end and is capable of being measured in a number of different ways.

Measurement of a process can always be done numerically, from the perspective of cost, time, or energy expended to accomplish the process for a number of clients or participants. It can also be measured from the perspective of the quality of the work or quality of benefit to the client that has been accomplished.

> A *key process* is an important set of linked activities in your program or organization that combine to produce a component of a product or service for a client or stakeholder.

Technology is often, but not always, used to collect data to improve the efficiency and effectiveness of a process. Processes are improved in many different ways, almost always by people inquiring about their effectiveness and efficiency.

Practice does not make perfect. You can continue to practice bad habits and stay the same or even get worse. Only *perfect* practice makes perfect. But perfection for most of us is a long way off. So how about making progress? How about just getting better?

That is what process improvement is about. Getting better. Getting better at serving our clients, getting better at stewarding our resources, getting better at changing people's lives, getting better at making a positive impact in the community.

Another critical component of process improvement and working smarter is innovation. If we are not getting better, we are actually getting worse, because the rest of the world is getting better all around us.

> *It's not enough to do your best; you must know what to do, then do your best.*
>
> –W. Edwards Deming (1900–1993), Statistician and Business Strategist

A few years ago, I was headed out on a canoe camping trip in the Boundary Waters Canoe Area Wilderness of northern Minnesota. There were a couple of pieces of camping equipment I needed to replace, so I set out looking online for the best prices and quality.

Two different sporting goods companies carried the products I wanted at almost exactly the same price and shipping cost. One company promised three-day delivery, and the other said it would take a week to ten days. It was still two weeks before the camping trip, but you can guess which company got my business. Not too long ago, a three-day delivery of product as standard operating procedure would have been considered impossible. Many companies now ship a product within twelve hours of the order. Businesses are getting better at what they do every day. They must, or they will go out of business.

While your nonprofit does not have a process to deliver camping supplies, the question is how frequently do you review the process of delivery of programs for effectiveness? Are the processes working the way you want them to? Are they timely and efficient? Let's take a look.

> *Every process is perfectly designed to achieve exactly the results it gets.*
>
> –Dr. Don Berwick (born 1946), CEO, Institute for Healthcare Improvement

The following is a list of potential innovation and quality improvement practices, processes, actions, and opportunities in a nonprofit organization. They are captured within the level/color where they most appropriately fit along a continuum of legal requirements to excellent practices. Determine your adherence to the practice or action with a check in the box.

STOP Red–Stop (Legal Requirements)

There are no legal requirements for having effective and efficient processes or procedures in a nonprofit organization or for fixing processes that are broken. It is even true, and very sad, that in some instances, poor and antiquated processes are still required by funders and the organization is bound to follow them to obtain operating resources.

I remember a comic strip from the '40s and '50s, "There Oughta Be a Law," written by Al Fagaly. The strip garnered laughs about outlandish inefficiencies in operations and processes of organizations and the extremes some people would take to accomplish a task. Maybe the comic "Dilbert" or the sitcom *The Office* fulfills that need to laugh at ourselves and these processes today.

What makes these so funny is not only the sarcasm but also the truth embedded in the outlandish. So while we have witnessed much truth in the inefficiencies and ineffectiveness of some nonprofit processes, there is probably nothing illegal about it.

CAUTION Yellow–Caution (Principled Ethics and Transparency)

✓	Practice or Action
	Best practices of other similar programs or those indicated as exemplary at the state or federal level have been utilized in the design and delivery of program processes.
	Programs have been developed and revised to meet client/customer/stakeholder needs in your locality and for your demographic, not just adopted from another organization.

✓	Practice or Action
	Activities, programs, and services are measured in some way such that management can determine that they are operating reasonably well toward offering the best possible outputs and outcomes for clients.
	Processes (activities) are measured in some fashion relative to the timeliness of their delivery, product quality, or satisfaction for clients.

While there may not be legal issues, there are ethical issues. Wasting resources as a result of inefficiency or ineffectiveness might be considered stealing from your funders, stakeholders, and clients. Providing more efficient services or programs means that everyone benefits from ever-diminishing or restricted resources.

Green–Go (Good Work/Growing Capacity)

✓	Practice or Action
	All staff members understand the reason why they perform the activity the way it is done.
	A set of measures is in place to determine the effectiveness of the activity or process and its efficiency. Data are regularly collected and analyzed.
	Suggestions from staff and stakeholders for improving activities or work processes are regularly gathered and used to improve the process or flow of work.
	All staff members have the ability and are encouraged to change a process if they feel they are able to make it work better.
	Innovations in program design or delivery have been made recently.
	The organization applies for and or works toward outside accreditation of its work as a means of improving its systems and processes.

The growing organization understands the power of looking at the way work gets done and the processes that support those benefits to people and the community.

Blue Ribbon (Superior Quality)

✓	Practice or Action
	The most important (often called critical or key) processes in our programs and organization have been identified in a formal way.
	The process of delivery of programs is formally and systematically reviewed regularly for effectiveness and efficiency.

✓	Practice or Action
	Parameters of accomplishment have been established for key processes. They take into account both the efficiency of the process and the effectiveness of the process. It is expected that those measurements are achieved regularly.
	Subprocesses have been articulated for each key process and are regularly measured as well.
	Improvements in process are expected by leadership and accomplished routinely and regularly.
	Measures are in place to determine the efficiency of the activity or process, and data are regularly collected.
	There is a regularly scheduled quality review of all critical and key processes of the organization.
	No staff member is penalized for an attempt to make a positive change in a process, even if it does not succeed.
	Our activity, program, and service processes are measured in relationship to outputs and outcomes to determine that the best possible outcomes are being accomplished for our clients.
	Measurement is designed to regulate and control the delivery of programs for consistency and effectiveness when delivered by different staff/volunteers or in different locations.

Not content to rest on the basic understanding of how effective and efficient processes contribute to their accomplishments, a Blue Ribbon organization strives for improvement in those processes. For example: The fundraising process is probably a key process in your organization. There should be expectations of timeliness and cost containment for that process. They might be measured by cost to raise a dollar or fundraising goals as a percentage of revenue. You pick them apart and expect improvements on a regular basis. There is no saying "good enough." There is an ongoing expectation of delivering services better and more quickly and with fewer resources than previously. The Blue Ribbon organization will also be looking at subprocesses. In the fundraising example above, the grantwriting process might be considered a subprocess and be measured in similar ways as the broader fundraising process. That grantwriting process may be further divided into research, identification, contact, writing, submission, and stewardship processes. Each subprocess can be measured and improved.

Gold Cup (Preeminent Practice/Excellence)

✓	Practice or Action
	Being known as an organization having the highest standards of quality of product or service is important for all staff and volunteers.

✓	Practice or Action
	Innovations in your program design and in processes of delivery are both expected and regularly made.
	Key processes and subprocesses are established, written, documented, measured, and communicated so that they are consistently delivered by different staff at different times or in different locations.
	In order to ensure that processes are accomplished in the same way, all people involved with the process receive regular training on the important aspects of the process and the standards of measurement.
	Following documentation of a positive change in the process, the change is adopted by all staff at all locations where the process is used. Staff willingly accepts the new process revisions.
	Programs are developed, measured, and regularly revised to meet client/customer/stakeholder needs as indicated by the client or customer themselves. Clients and customers are often involved in program design and revisions.
	Other organizations and leaders look to your organization as exemplary and regularly solicit advice about improving their own processes and outcomes.
	The organization expects that other organizations with which it works to fulfill its mission are also improving their processes and not inhibiting it from continually getting better.

Noting the items in the preeminent practice category will cause some people to rail against the seeming impersonal nature of delivery of services when they are regulated and consistency is expected. *Au contraire!* Consistency of purpose and service delivery means fairness and equity… as much as it is possible in human services. It also allows for the assurance that all important aspects of the process are accomplished, none are forgotten, and accuracy is maintained, which in turn, allows for the most opportunity for interpersonal connection.

The identification, measurement, and improvement of internal work processes is critical to effective and efficient delivery of services. If you don't know how something works, it is very difficult to manage it, fix it if broken, or replicate it another time. Understanding your activities and flow of work is critical.

To Recap

- ◆ As a leader, you must understand the process of your work and how to track its performance.

- ◆ Measuring how you do your work is crucial to helping your organization improve.

- ◆ Organizational quality begins with leadership. Being excellent at delivering your product or service doesn't just happen. You need to really want it, work at it, and lead it.

Chapter Ten

Deadly Saying Seven: "We're Doing Pretty Well This Year"

IN THIS CHAPTER

- The difference between your good work and good results
- Questions about results
- Results: outcomes, impact, and financials

The difference between saying we are doing "pretty well" and actually sharing the changes in people's lives and benefits to the community from your work is the difference between survival and growth as an organization. Positive performance is no longer about providing a service or program. It is about what happens as a result of the service or program to advance the quality of life for those who interact with your organization.

Differing Opinions of "Doing Well"

I was contracted by a local foundation to assist a rural community food shelf to develop a fundraising plan. The problem, as I was told, was that the food shelf was running out of money and would not be able to give out Thanksgiving baskets because of the increase in demand over the previous months.

I was welcomed in the church basement with coffee and wonderful treats by the dozen or so white-haired women who comprised the board of directors of the food shelf. We began in earnest to delve into the issues. We discussed where funds came from, how fundraising had taken place, current food shelf usage, and a variety of topics.

But no one seemed to know how many donors there were or how much had been given. The person responsible for recording gifts and thanking donors was not there that morning. I was told, though, that she had a good system of three-by-five cards that had all the donor information. There was some money in the bank, in a couple of checking accounts and several CDs, but the exact numbers were not immediately available. The treasurer had all that information, but she would need to go through her ledger books to figure it out.

When I asked about the budget, I was told they did not have one. "We'll need to develop a budget," I said.

"Why?" someone asked.

"Because we need to understand about your revenues and expenses in order to show your donors what you need," I stated.

"Well, we can't put a budget together," the board chair countered. "We don't know from one month to the next what will come in or how much we will give out. A budget is not really truthful. It is really just a lie."

Several community members representing the clergy, businesses, service groups, etc., joined us for lunch and we discussed how the community could help raise both funds and awareness. A local business owner indicated that she had never been asked to support the shelf, but could. A bank president indicated he had worked as a board member of a food shelf in another locality before recently moving into town and would be willing to help. A local member of the clergy shared that the church has always been supportive, but the congregation was not aware of the increase in usage.

The discussion with the board continued after lunch. The board seemed unwilling to ask previous donors for help. Members were certain that it was breech of protocol to share data on historical giving or amounts with me, an outsider. They felt it violated privacy issues to share an anonymous client story. They had retained no data about in-kind contributions of food or food disbursements past the end of each month of operations. After they submitted their monthly report to the state food bank, they tossed the information.

After returning to my office and investigating further, I discovered via the organization's IRS 990 tax form that they had revenues and expenses the previous year of about $50,000 and had cash reserves of more than $87,000. I heard later that there was concern expressed by one member of the board that if the community knew how much money this nonprofit had in the bank, people would stop giving to the food shelf.

And when the community did find out, the Thanksgiving baskets were provided, as were special meals for the holidays. The community also demanded changes in the structure of the organization and the membership of the board of directors.

The board members thought the organization was doing pretty well. When the community learned the facts, they did not share that same opinion. While financially stable, the food shelf was truly not serving the community well.

We Have All the Stats

Joyce was just coming back to the office after having lunch with a donor. As the director of development, she was used to frustration and rejection. But this was different. The donor was Rosa Garcia, the owner of Latina Muchacha, a corporate benefactor that had provided multiyear funding for the start-up and expansion of the Latina Wellness Program. This was the fifth year of funding from Rosa, and the meeting had been to ask for another three years of support.

The discussion had been lively and informing. Joyce talked about the work that had been done, about the staff, the facilities they had improved, and the significant number of women and children who had been through the program. Some of them had been regular participants for over four years. Joyce had all the statistics: how many women had been screened, for what conditions, treatment recommendations, cooking class attendance, times spent with the nutritionist and trainer, and on, and on.

But it didn't seem to be enough for Rosa. She wanted to know if there had been health improvements in any of the participants. She wanted to know about changes in eating habits, nutritional meals for the kids, exercise, and athletic participation for the girls. Rosa asked if the average BMI of the women had decreased and if fewer of them were smoking. "What about the incidence of diabetes?" she asked. "Has there been any change over the years?"

Rosa had not outright turned down the request for continued funding. She had said she'd think about it.

"So many difficult questions," Joyce complained to Tom, her executive, after telling him the story.

"We put out a report on program participation," Tom griped. "We have all the stats. What more information do they want?"

Revenue Forecasting

The third-quarter treasurer's report was pretty much the same as last quarter and the quarter before that. Expenses had been right about the same as revenue. Donations were down a bit, but a new operational grant made up for that. Program expenses seemed to be on the rise, but nothing unmanageable within current budgeted projections. What was frustrating to Francis, the board chair, was that this was the year when the strategic goal was to put at least 10 percent of the year's revenue into reserve. Setting up a reserve should have happened years ago, but this was the year when it seemed financially feasible. But it sure didn't look hopeful anymore. "And when we prepared the budget, I thought things looked pretty good for this year." He muttered to himself, "I guess we'll need to try again."

Questions about Your Outcomes and Impact

- ◆ Are your results (outputs and outcomes) positive and moving in a preferential direction?

> **observation**
> There is a big difference between counting the number of wonderful activities you do and identifying the changes in people's lives resulting from those activities.

- What are your financial and fundraising results?

- Are your financial results acceptable? Do you have a ready and sufficient reserve?

- Do you measure your efficiency? Are you aware of the actual costs of individual programs or other components of your organization?

- Do you measure return on investment, cost to raise a dollar, or other internal, analytical measures of efficiency?

- What actions have you taken to correct poor efficiency or effectiveness?

- Do you consider any leading indicators of positive or negative results, or are all your measures lagging in nature?

Results: Outcome, Impact, and Financial Results

Most nonprofits do report on their programs and activities. Many, unfortunately, stop there. They stop with the report on activities and the number of people served. They do so because they believe those activities are accomplishing the best for their clients and stakeholders, and it may be all that a funder expects. Annual reports are able to share the "stories" of success. There is that individual who overcame great obstacles with the help of your activities. That one wonderful and highly acclaimed performance made the headlines.

But, overall, are you having a positive outcome—making a difference in the lives of your clients? Have you created a positive impact in the community? If you do not know, then how do you know that you are doing the right things? How do you know that all those activities are actually the right ones to be doing?

> **definition**
> The outcome of a program is the change in someone's life as a result of participating in that program. There is a big difference between counting the number of good activities you do and the changes in people's lives as a result of those activities.

What are the results of your efforts?

How good are you at stewarding your resources? Are you doing a good job financially? Are your facilities adequate and up to date? Are your technologies current, and do they enable you to function effectively and efficiently? In order to have positive outcomes, your infrastructure also needs to be functioning well.

This final deadly saying challenges you to answer a set of questions I initially heard raised by Dr. Mark Blazey at a Minnesota Performance Excellence Network training session. He asked the following set of questions:

1. Are you any good?
2. Are you getting better?
3. How do you know?

Using data to prove that you are good and getting better is a critical component of fundraising. It is a factor in staff and volunteer retention and client satisfaction.

Let's consider, then, the measures you use to determine and report your performance. We will consider the collection of that data, frequency, and methods.

We need to think about how those data are stored and retrieved in order for information to be obtained from the data.

And then the data need to be analyzed and conclusions drawn that will be able to assist leaders in managing the programs and organization.

Finally, we can't operate on a hand-to-mouth basis. If the programs and services really do good things for people, then we want to be sure they are around to continue to meet those needs. Our finances must be secure and our infrastructure solid. This takes consistent and strong leadership and strategic foresight and planning.

I remember the time in the sector when it was acceptable to end the year in a deficit financial condition. The feeling in some social service organizations was that a financial loss indicated the significance of the need for the services and programs the organization provided and provided a basis for demonstrating the need for additional funding.

Then, later, there was a movement in the sector that encouraged "zero-based budgeting." The intent was to plan your expenses based on conservative revenue projections. This would allow the organization to end the year with a zero sum, spending the same amount in the year that it accomplished in income.

Neither of those options proved operationally beneficial for organizations or for the clients and stakeholders they served.

Now it is considered appropriate that a healthy organization, one with solid governance and effective leadership, will demonstrate financial reserves and programmatic accomplishments that will carry it through in the event of societal or economic downturns.

The following is a list of performance management practices, actions, and expectations in a nonprofit organization. They are detailed within the color/symbol level where they are most appropriate. Determine your acceptance or adherence to the practice or action with a check in the box.

🛑 STOP — Red–Stop (Legal Requirements)

✓	Practice or Action
	All members of the board actively participate in reviewing organizational reports and documents.
	Minutes of the board meetings and any committee of the board are taken and accurately reflect discussion and actions of the group.
	Members of the board understand the books, records, documents, policies, and procedures of record keeping and data collection.
	Your organization complies with all state and federal requirements for filings of employment and tax reporting on the timelines required by the government, including the payment of sales, FICA, payroll, and other taxes as required.
	IRS 990 tax statements are submitted in a timely fashion and with full understanding of the board of directors.
	A professional external audit of finances and financial protocols is conducted annually or as required.
	All restricted and donor funds are tracked and accounted for in the financial reports and are used only as directed by the donor.
	Financial reports and results are made available to the public in an easily understood fashion.

Legal requirements for performance measurement are focused primarily, if not totally, on financial results and sharing them with the appropriate authorities. There are, however, some requirements of the members of the board of directors and organizational leaders that are important for appropriate management and reporting of financial data.

⚠️ CAUTION — Yellow–Caution (Principled Ethics and Transparency)

✓	Practice or Action
	Programmatic results (outputs and outcomes) are positive and moving in a preferential direction.
	Customers are generally satisfied with the services or products they receive from you.
	Financial results are acceptable.
	Board members and staff are aware of the actual costs of individual programs or other components of your organization.
	Results of programming efforts and outcomes are made available to the community at least annually in a proactive fashion.

The ethical and transparent organization is open to scrutiny from the community. It actively provides information so that the community can assess its performance and support it. It demonstrates the value it provides for the community in terms of providing services that would otherwise need to be provided by taxpayers. At a minimum, an annual audit and annual report of activities is provided to the board of directors and the community.

Financially, the organization is balanced and meeting program and mission expenses with sufficient revenues. The organization does not attempt to detract or infringe, either from a service perspective or financially, on other community organizations.

GO Green–Go (Good Work/Growing Capacity)

✓	Practice or Action
	Financial and fundraising results are positive and a reserve is available and being expanded.
	Customer/client satisfaction results are positive and are regularly collected and tracked for changes.
	Return on investment is measured for individual programs and is positive.
	Cost to raise a dollar is determined and tracked and is good.
	Internal measures of efficiency, such as time to complete a task or program, or people served per staff full-time equivalent, are captured and used for improvement.
	Program effectiveness measures (outcomes) are collected and tracked for use by management.
	Management actions have been taken recently to correct poor efficiency or effectiveness.
	Your organization has a ready and sufficient cash reserve appropriate to your revenue types and flow. Generally, this constitutes a minimum of three months' operating cash.
	You track and measure your process efficiency—the time or other resources it takes to accomplish a routine task of a program or your organization.
	Effectiveness of services, or client outcomes, is measured, reported regularly, and positive in nature.
	Customer satisfaction is measured regularly and is positive in nature.
	Criticisms or complaints are handled quickly and to the satisfaction of the customer, participant, or stakeholder.
	Your organization is beginning to utilize some measures that are leading or future oriented as a means of predicting future performance.
	Operational measures are tied to the strategic goals of the organization.

The good and growing organization is looking beyond the past and immediate future and considering its role in improving the community. It is looking at how its outcomes for people are changing social structures or conditions. Its financial situation is balanced, and there is a solid reserve being established so that shifts in funding will not negatively impact services to clients or the community.

Both clients and community are well satisfied with the programming, and results are generally positive. Management looks both internally and externally for means to improve its products and services.

Blue Ribbon (Superior Quality)

✓	Practice or Action
	An operating cash reserve equivalent to six to twelve months of expenses is available for use if required.
	Your organization is sufficiently stable to accomplish new programming and innovate without reliance on outside support, i.e., a grant is not always required to begin a new program.
	Measures of the quality and quantity of inputs, activities, outputs, outcomes, and impact are measured against predetermined goals.
	Trends for all programmatic measures, including inputs, activities, outputs, and outcomes, are monitored and used by program or organizational leaders for management purposes.
	Appropriate levels (controls) of accomplishment are established for a variety of program and organizational measurements.
	Important measures are integrated throughout the organization and understood and supported by all staff and volunteers.
	Staff and volunteers understand how their actions and activities impact accomplishment of organizational outputs and, hence, the mission and impact of the organization on the community.
	The board has a process in place to measure its own effectiveness and efficiency.

The Blue Ribbon organization is both competent and vigilant. Financial measures are positive and revenue streams are diverse and consistent. Innovation in programming is regularly implemented in ways that offer new opportunities for clients and the community. The Blue Ribbon organization continually seeks to improve the outcomes for clients and its impact on the community.

Data are used significantly in the organization to make decisions and direct activities. Staff understands and contributes to good data collection and analysis.

Gold Cup (Preeminent Practice/Excellence)

✓	Practice or Action
	Staff and volunteer performance and incentives are tied directly to accomplishment of organizational measures and goals that are established to support the organizational mission.
	Your organization benchmarks its goals and actual accomplishments against a set of standards for best-in-class organizations doing similar activities or providing similar products or services.
	The culture or your organization is such that all staff and volunteers understand the need for measurement but also recommend opportunities and methods for capturing new and appropriate measures.
	Your organization shares its results with other organizations as a means of benefit to the overall client base and community.
	Other organizations look to you for advice and recommendation on best practices of measurement and management.

Very little happens in a Gold Cup organization that is not validated with data and solid analysis. It is a data-driven organization, with the staff, volunteers, and board supporting and expecting data to be used by everybody.

Financial results are consistent and positive, and reserves and plans for unexpected changes in the economy or programming are in place to guard against organizational problems. More than likely, there is a significant operational (perhaps board-restricted) reserve or perhaps an endowment.

The organization serves as a benchmark for other organizations—nonprofit, for-profit, *and* public—sharing its information to benefit the work of others on behalf of its clientele.

Because the social sector does not have the ability to tax its clients or generally charge for the full cost of its products or services but instead relies on the generosity of the community, performance in the social sector needs to be better than in the public or private sector. It is for this reason that the measurement and management of your nonprofit's performance is so critical.

To Recap

- There is a significant difference between doing good work and having good results.
- As a leader, you need to determine your results in order to establish goals to get better.
- Your programmatic and organizational results need to be shared with the community. After all, they are your owners.

Chapter Eleven

In the Beginning, or Once Upon a Time...

IN THIS CHAPTER

- Federal fiscal management
- Principles and practices of nonprofit excellence
- Standards of accountability
- Donor Bill of Rights
- Total quality management and criteria for performance excellence

As a new executive director of a small, multifaceted human services nonprofit organization in rural Minnesota, I raised my hand and accepted the responsibility of being the fiscal agent for a million-dollar federal grant awarded to a consortium of organizations in our community.

What I did not discern in accepting that responsibility was that the policies and practices of my small nonprofit would need to grow up very quickly. Before the release of any money, an IRS auditor spent three days in my office looking at almost everything we did and how we did it. While there were some fiscal and management practices we were doing well, there were, as they say, "opportunities for improvement." So we set out to improve many of our processes and document our informal policies and practices.

That opportunity to drink from the fire hose had a significant impact on my future view of fiscal and human resource management issues. It made me aware of both the very real reasons that a policy is necessary and the best practices available for use.

Principles and Practices of Nonprofit Excellence

As a developing executive director, I was gleaning bits of information about leadership and management from conferences, seminars, learning circles, mentors, university courses, and federal auditors as previously noted. Then I was privileged to be included in a select committee of the Minnesota Council of Nonprofits (MCN), which worked alongside the Charities Review Council and MAP for Nonprofits to establish a set of principles and recommended practices for effective nonprofit management. This framing was the output of discussions beginning as early as 1993 with hundreds of nonprofit leaders across the state of Minnesota. Over months of meetings, the group identified the categories and set recommendations for practice to one of the first such documents in the nation. *Principles and Practices for Nonprofit Excellence: A guide for nonprofit board members, managers and staff*, the draft document, reviewed by leaders of hundreds of nonprofit organizations in Minnesota, was adopted by resolution of the membership in October 1998.

> There is nothing like having a federal auditor spend three days in your office going over your policies, procedures, books, and record keeping. He let us know very quickly what we were doing appropriately and what needed work in order to be considered an acceptable recipient of federal moneys and act as the fiscal agent for a federal grant. That was my experience back in 1992. There is no equivocating with a federal auditor!
>
> **stories from the real world**

The original document was revised and amended in 2004 to include additional categories and clarification of others. Along with previous and new committee members, I was again privileged to serve on this committee. Adopted in March 2005 by the membership of MCN, the manuscript has aided thousands of nonprofit leaders to capture the essence of the things they need to do in order to be legal, better, and yes, excellent. *Principles and Practices of Nonprofit Excellence* has served as a blueprint for dozens of other state nonprofit associations that have penned and adopted their own documents importing the ways and means for nonprofit organizational improvement. It is currently undergoing another revision and should be released in early 2014.

> *Principles and Practices of Nonprofit Excellence* can be found on the website of the Minnesota Council of Nonprofits at minnesotanonprofits.org/nonprofit-resources/principles-and-practices or in summary fashion in **Appendix A** of this book. Its third edition is expected to be released early in 2014.
>
> **principle**

Standards of Accountability

The second set of nonprofit management concepts was introduced to me as a "here is something we should really do" statement by one of my board members. Since a board member's recommendation is not to be taken lightly, I investigated the Charities Review Council's standards for being considered an "accountable" nonprofit. My organization was a card or two shy of a full house on the expectations of the

Good Nonprofit Housekeeping Seal of Approval, so we worked hard the next year to obtain the affirmation. The expectations of the council were reasonable, but they still challenged us to revise some internal processes and establish some protocols. Our organization had to watch its finances and reporting as well as its management policies and procedures.

In the latest decades, a number of entities have provided a watchdog-like surveillance of nonprofit organizations in an attempt to give prospective donors the summary financial and management information they need and want prior to committing their own resources to a cause. GuideStar and the Better Business Bureau are just two others of similar persuasion to the Charities Review Council whose intent it is to aid the uninformed about the organization to which they intend to contribute.

In most recent years, the Charities Review Council has adopted a slightly different perspective and now prefers to identify itself as a *guide dog* helping nonprofit organizations improve and meet the standards rather than the noisier and more aggressive *watchdog* variety. So it is appropriate that the essence of its guidelines finds inclusion in this book. Simply sounding the alert is valuable only if there are means available to protect and defend community resources. Strengthening the leadership and management practice of the nonprofit organization is a much more positive approach than barking loudly after community resources are misused and people's lives devastated.

> Both *watchdogs* and *guide dogs* have their place in the world of nonprofit practice. One points out what is wrong; the other directs toward better policy and practice. I tend to prefer the latter.
>
> **definition**

A Donor Bill of Rights

As I engaged the process of obtaining the credential of a Certified Fundraising Executive (CFRE), the document *A Donor Bill of Rights* made an impression on my personal work. Developed by the Association of Fundraising Professionals (AFP), the Association for Healthcare Philanthropy (AHP), the Council for Advancement and Support of Education (CASE), and the Giving Institute, it lays out ten things that donors have the right to expect from the organizations to which they have or are considering donating. The document has become a standard for donors and organizations in a philanthropic relationship. It bears posting on the wall of every nonprofit leader and fundraiser.

> Check out the AFP's *Donor Bill of Rights* at the Association of Fundraising Professionals at afpnet.org/ethics/enforcementdetail.cfm?itemnumber=3359.
>
> **practical tip**

For even greater detail, you might investigate the *"Code of Ethical Principles and Standards"* of the Association of Fundraising Professionals. Adopted in 1964 and amended in 2007, this second document provides some excellent recommendations for any individual or organization involved in raising funds and other resources from the public.

Total Quality Management

Dr. Jerry Spicer, the insightful former CEO of the Hazelden Foundation, pulled and prodded me into the arena of total quality management and process improvement. Like most of the leadership and management of the organization at the time, I did not go willingly.

It is hard work to collect data, manage data, and turn data into information that can be analyzed to make decisions. Most of us liked our comfortable intuitive decision-making processes. Now we were expected to chart our key processes, convene improvement teams, fix broken procedures, measure what we did, work smarter, and actually care about what our customers thought! What on earth was he expecting of us? After all, we were treating the chemically dependent; we didn't need a balanced scorecard or data dashboard to do it!

Nevertheless, it was amazing how much better we actually got. Moreover, I'm happy to report that Jerry's not-so-subtle encouragement helped me learn much about the work of an organization and how it can improve to do a better job for its clients.

Criteria for Performance Excellence

Part of Jerry's encouragement was for me to become a member of the board of evaluators for the Minnesota Council for Quality, now the Performance Excellence Network (PEN). PEN bases its efforts on the Baldrige National Quality Program and its Criteria for Performance Excellence. This program finds its history in the establishment of the federal Malcolm Baldrige National Quality Improvement Act of 1987.

As one of more than forty active statewide organizations working to improve the business, education, health, and nonprofit organizations in their respective states, PEN follows the guidelines established at the national level for organizations seeking the most coveted Malcolm Baldrige Quality Award.

> Check out the Criteria for Performance Excellence at nist.gov/baldrige.
>
> *practical tip*

Serving as a quality evaluator with PEN allowed me the privilege of investigating educational, nonprofit, government, health, and profit organizations to see what makes them "excellent" and to help them find their opportunities for improvement. It provided an opportunity for me to look inside organizations that are striving to achieve excellence in their fields. They want to be good, and they endeavor to get better.

Investigating their efforts, commenting on what they have accomplished, and recommending opportunities for improvement based on the definitions of the standards of excellence has provided valuable insight for the ideas expressed in this book. More than that, however, it has infused the concepts of excellent striving for excellence a part of my hope and encouragement for the organizations of our sector.

Four documents—*Principles and Practices of Nonprofit Excellence* of the Minnesota Council of Nonprofits, the Charities Review Council's *Accountability Standards,* AFP's *Donor Bill of Rights,* and the National Baldrige Quality Program's *Criteria for Performance Excellence*—are the primary inspiration for this assessment offered for your investigation and work. Additional ideas and suggestions are included as a result of learning from my own mistakes, errors, and foolishness over the decades, or by way of real situations shared by some of my clients. Thoughtful insight originating from my peers and students is also embedded in these suggestions for you and your nonprofit organization.

To Recap

- If our nonprofit organizations are not getting better, they are getting worse. Just staying the same, doing the same things, and having the same results means the rest of the world is passing us by. Don't let it! Complacency is no longer an option.

- Nonprofit associations and social sector proponent groups have great tools for your use... use them.

- Getting better takes leadership that really wants to improve what its organization is doing. Want it!

Chapter Twelve

Leading a Healthy Organization

IN THIS CHAPTER

- ⇢ Lots of activity, but no outcomes
- ⇢ Ten recommendations for you and your nonprofit
- ⇢ Deadly sayings don't need to be deadly
- ⇢ Don't try to eat the whole elephant in one sitting

I sat across the table from the CEO of a well-respected chemical-dependency rehab and housing facility in a large metro area. He invited me to help investigate and implement some major-giving fundraising tactics. Government reimbursement for program operations was being reduced, and the CEO realized that something would need to change. They had never before had to seek significant fundraising to support their core programs. All the operational support had been from local and county payments for services. The program was operating at capacity and had a waiting list. The facility, which the organization had built a decade ago, was seeing some need for better upkeep, an indication to me that finances had been difficult for some time.

"So," I asked, after getting a tour of the facility, "how is the program doing?"

"Great," the CEO indicated, and then proceeded to show me the latest annual report with indications of the numbers of service recipients and a story about a client who went from the street, addicted to heroin, to a decent job and was moving into a house with his reunited family.

"That is a wonderful example," I said, "but what is your abstinence rate at six months? How about your recidivism rate? How many of the people who come through your door are actually getting better or find their living situations more positive following treatment?"

Looking at me with wide eyes and a blank expression, the CEO said, "We never had to worry about all that stuff. The county only asked about the number of people we were serving each month, so that's all our accountant has been gathering. We don't keep track of our clients after they leave. I don't think we have any way to get that information."

The conversation continued politely for another fifteen minutes. He surely thought that I was not a very good fundraiser, and I realized that he was not going to even try to gather the information needed to develop a solid case and approach major donors to ask for their support.

The story is both true and unfortunate. Most frequently, the lack of revenue or problems of raising funds is only symptomatic of other underlying and more significant issues. Problems of strategy, governance, leadership, or measurement and performance are preventing good fundraising from happening. This is borne out not only by my experience but will most likely resonate with you, especially if you have been tasked with raising new money for programs operating under the old pay-for-services mode of many counties.

Some readers looking for quick fixes and easy fundraising tactics will have put this book down chapters ago believing that all that planning, leadership, and measurement stuff was way too much work and effort for the simple problem they have... just needing a bit more revenue to offset the rising need demonstrated by their clients and stakeholders.

Ten Recommendations

But the fact that you are still here indicates an interest on your part to make changes of substance to the way you work and to demonstrate the results you accomplish. So consider these final thoughts and remarks as ideas in your quest for excellence.

1. Begin with the end in mind.

   Whether you are considering a change or improvement in an activity, key process, or organizational structure, think about the end result or outcome of the work you want to accomplish. When evaluating, determine who will use the information and for what purpose before you begin the process of gathering data. Invite as many others as possible to participate in the investigation.

2. Baby steps are often better.

   Someone once said that "the only person who likes change is a baby with a messy diaper." As a leader of a nonprofit organization, you are dealing with people. And people generally don't like change. Organizations, made up of many people, like change even less. Change takes dissatisfaction with the status quo, a vision of something better, believability, time, motivating energy, and hand-holding. Sometimes critical incidents necessitate swift change. Generally, slow and steady change, based on data, wins the race.

3. If it moves, measure it.

   My father came back from the US Navy after World War II with a phrase: "If it moves, salute it. If it doesn't, paint it!" So, if it moves, acknowledge it and measure its progress or change. It is only with good data that you will ever be able to make solid management decisions.

4. Demand measurement.

   Another evaluation consultant and I spent more than twelve months working with staff and leadership to establish an evaluation protocol for a culturally specific family services agency. The board had asked for it, the executive director wanted it, a foundation funded it, and the staff supported it. We set the process up so that it could be done within the scope of normal staff work activity and would not take significant time. During the process of our work, the executive director left for a new and challenging position.

   I happened to meet the new executive director at a conference a year or so later and inquired how the evaluation plan was working. He said he was hoping for some foundation funding to come through so he could get it started. I left the conversation frustrated and dejected. If he was not going to expect his staff to gather the data, it was never going to happen... additional funding or not.

5. Trust people to do good work.

   I haven't met many people who show up at work planning to do a lousy job. Most people I know want to perform their duties well and feel good about the work they do. So if something seems broken, look first for a problem in the process, not at the people performing the task.

   But what if you hired the wrong person for the job, I've been asked. Then you probably have a problem with the hiring process, not the person you hired. Think about it! The person is who she or he is. They just are not the right one for that particular job. It is a process problem, not a people problem.

6. Back up your fundraising story with outcome data.

   The greater competition there is for resources, the more important it is to be able to demonstrate the value of what you do for the individual and for the community. Counting activities or people through the door is no longer enough. Government funding is now paying for performance, and private donors are expecting positive change for people. You need to be able to document the data that indicate the value of what you do for people, their lives, and the community.

> *Three things are not long hidden: the sun, the moon, and the truth.*
>
> —Gautama Buddha (circa 500 BCE)

7. Even a questionable strategic plan is better than no plan at all.

   If you start working on a bad plan and measure it, the fact that it is a bad plan will soon become apparent. Not having a plan will give you no information at all about what you are doing or where you are going. Write a plan and work the plan. There is much written on the subject and many approaches. Most of them work if you use them. None of them work if you don't.

8. Get beyond the "I am the expert" attitude.

   Even if you have advanced academic degrees and decades of experience in your field, it is still your customers, clients, or stakeholders who know best what they need and want. Listen to them first, second, and last. Use your knowledge to augment rather than to supersede what they tell you.

9. Transparency is crucial.

   As an organization that is owned and supported by the community, it is important to be open and truthful with that community. Yes, there is risk in being transparent and telling your community about who you are, what you do, and how you do it. However, the consequences for not being transparent are more significant and detrimental.

10. Never stop! Never!

    Once you stop getting better, you start to die. That is a fact of biology. It is also a fact of organizational life. The way to discovery about growth and positive change is to measure and track what is happening. Evaluate what you do. It can only be a positive endeavor.

Deadly Sayings Don't Need to Be Deadly

The seven sayings are deadly only if ignored and left unanswered. Your reaction and response to hearing the sayings is the critical difference between a healthy and growing nonprofit and an organization that will ultimately stumble and possibly fall. You, the leader, need to take action!

Don't Try to Eat the Whole Elephant at One Sitting

A friend of mine once shared the following recipe with me.

While I have not had the opportunity to try the recipe, I'm sure it would be tasty. But I'm also quite sure I would not prepare the recipe just for my dinner.

> **Elephant Stew**
>
> Ingredients:
>
> - 1 medium-sized elephant
> - 3 fifty-gallon containers of savory broth
> - 600 pounds of assorted fresh vegetables, chopped
> - Salt and pepper to taste
> - 2 rabbits (optional)
>
> Directions:
>
> - Cut elephant into one-inch cubes.
> - Using large kettles, simmer equal parts elephant and vegetables with enough broth to cover.
> - Cook until tender, stirring regularly.
>
> Preparation time:
>
> - 2–3 days depending on available help
>
> Cooking time:
>
> - 36–48 hours
>
> Serves:
>
> - 3,000
>
> Note: If more than three thousand people are expected, add the rabbits, but do this only if necessary, as most people do not like to find hare in their stew.

It can be very defeatist to contemplate eating a whole elephant yourself in one sitting. It can be just as defeatist to contemplate undertaking all the activities suggested in this book. So don't. Think about it in small-sized bowls with lots of friends.

You don't have to, nor should you, undertake all of the activities suggested in this book in the next week, month, or even year. This is especially true if yours is a small shop of only a couple of people. Think strategically about which tactics need to be undertaken first and which will need to wait. But don't wait to start. Do something now.

To Recap

- Consider the ten recommendations for leading your nonprofit as springboards for organizational improvement.
- The deadly sayings don't need to be deadly if you pay attention and work smart.
- Don't try to eat the whole elephant in one sitting. Take it a little at a time. Make selective and smart changes.

Appendix A

Principles and Practices of Nonprofit Excellence

The Principles and Practices for Nonprofit Excellence are based on the fundamental values of quality, responsibility, and accountability. The ten characteristic accountability principles distinguish the nonprofit sector from government and the business sector. The 133 management practices provide specific guidelines for individual organizations to evaluate and improve their operations, governance, human resources, advocacy, financial management, and fundraising.

Role in Society

Nonprofits are obligated to understand their role as entities that engage and inspire individuals and communities for public benefit, and to conduct their activities with transparency, integrity, and accountability.

Governance

A nonprofit's board of directors is responsible for defining the organization's mission and for providing overall leadership and strategic direction to the organization.

Planning

Nonprofits have a duty to engage in sound planning, define a clear vision for the future, and specify strategies, goals, and objectives for plan implementation.

Transparency and Accountability

Nonprofits should regularly and openly convey information to the public about their mission, activities, accomplishments, and decision-making processes. Information from a nonprofit organization should be easily accessible to the public and should create external visibility, public understanding, and trust in the organization.

Fundraising

Nonprofits should adopt clear policies for fundraising activities to ensure responsible use of funds and open, transparent communication with contributors and other constituents.

Financial Management

Nonprofits must comply with all legal financial requirements and should adhere to sound accounting principles that produce reliable financial information, ensure fiscal responsibility, and build public trust.

Human Resources

Nonprofit organizations should place a high priority on exercising fair and equitable practices that attract and retain qualified volunteers and employees. Nonprofits have an obligation to adhere to all applicable employment laws and to provide a safe and productive work environment.

Civic Engagement and Public Policy

To the extent possible, nonprofit organizations should engage constituents in public policy and advocacy activities as a means to fulfilling their missions and promoting community interests.

Strategic Alliances

Nonprofits should initiate and promote cooperation and coordination between a variety of entities to avoid unnecessary duplication of services and to maximize the resources available to the communities they serve.

Evaluation

Nonprofits should regularly measure their performance against a clear set of goals and objectives. They should share this information with their constituents and the public and use it to continually improve the quality of their processes, programs and activities.

Principles and Practices for Nonprofit Excellence reprinted with permission of Minnesota Council of Nonprofits, Copyright © 2013 Minnesota Council of Nonprofits

Appendix B

Samples of National and State Standards of Excellence

Following are examples of standards for excellence:

- Independent Sector, independentsector.org/compendium_of_standards
- The National Association of Nonprofits, councilofnonprofits.org/resources/resources-type/principles-and-practices

Many state associations of nonprofit organizations have developed their own standards of accountability or standards of excellence. Here are just a few of these:

- Maryland Nonprofits, marylandnonprofits.org/dnn/strengthen/standardsforexcellence.aspx
- Pennsylvania Association of Nonprofit Organizations, pano.org/standards-for-excellence
- Alabama Association of Nonprofits, alabamanonprofits.org/standards-for-excellence-program.php
- Iowa Nonprofit Resource Center, inrc.continuetolearn.uiowa.edu/pandp/default.asp
- Colorado Nonprofit Association, coloradononprofits.org/help-desk-resources/principles-practices

Appendix C

Template for Operational Planning

Goal/objective (this comes from your strategic plan and should be SMART—specific, measurable, acceptable, realistic, and time-bound): _____

_____

_____

Assumptions/external factors: _____

_____

_____

What Key Tactics and/or Related Activities Will Be Done?	Who Will Do It?	When Will It Be Done?	How Much Will It Cost?	How Will It Be Measured?	Status/Comments
1.					
2.					
3.					
4.					
5.					

Repeat table for each new goal or objective.

Index

A

accountability, 10–11, 103–4
AFP's Donor Bill of Rights, 105, 107
assessment, 5, 7, 9, 11, 46, 68, 76, 107
  organizational, 68
  tool, 11–12
Association for Healthcare Philanthropy (AHP), 105
Association of Fundraising Professionals (AFP), 32, 105

B

Baldrige National Quality Program, 106
Blue Ribbon, 9–10, 20, 34–35, 47, 58, 68, 77, 89–90, 100
board, 4, 11, 17, 19, 21, 24–27, 29–37, 39–40, 42–43, 47–48, 58, 63, 66, 73, 75–76, 93–94, 98–101, 106, 111
  involvement, 32
  leadership, 34
  meetings, 23, 31–32, 66, 98
    minutes, 29
  policies, 34
  reviews, 20, 35
budget, 2, 25, 29, 39, 42, 49, 62, 73, 94–95
  annual, 29, 47
business community, 54
bylaws, 29

C

capacity, organizational, 11, 28–29, 34, 36, 43, 47, 78, 109
CEO, 11, 27–28, 30–31, 33, 35, 62, 88, 106, 109–10
Certified Fundraising Executive (CFRE), 105
charitable registration laws, 18
Charities Review Council, 104–5
clients, 2–3, 5, 7–8, 16, 19–20, 22, 24–25, 27–28, 30–32, 37, 40, 43, 46, 49, 51–61, 63–66, 69–70, 73–77, 83–84, 86–87, 89–91, 96–97, 100–101, 106–7, 109–10, 112
client satisfaction, 51, 54, 56, 59, 97
community, 5, 7, 13–17, 19–22, 25–27, 31–32, 34, 36–38, 40, 42, 44–49, 54–57, 59, 64, 66–67, 69, 73–74, 77–78, 87, 89, 93–94, 96, 98–101, 103, 111–12
  impact, 10, 69
  members, 8, 94
  relations, 57
  resources, 21, 47, 105
  stakeholders, 46
  support, 14, 19
constituents, 41, 44–47, 49, 54–55, 58
contributions, 39, 41–42, 48, 53, 84
core values, 20, 46
Criteria for Performance Excellence, 106

culture, 13, 38, 56, 60, 68–69, 73–74, 77, 101
  organizational, 16, 71, 79
customers, 7, 53–56, 58–59, 99

D

data collection, 64, 68–69, 98
Deming, W. Edwards, 86–87
development directors, 40, 83
directors, 4, 25, 27, 29–37, 40–42, 47–48, 52, 58, 62, 66, 72, 75–76, 93–95, 98–99
dissatisfaction, 56–58, 110
diversity, 26, 76–78
Donor Bill of Rights, 103, 105, 107
donors, 3, 8, 10, 16, 18, 22, 24, 27, 29–30, 32–33, 46–48, 51, 55–59, 66, 84, 93–95, 98, 105
  stewardship, 32, 55

E

effectiveness, 2, 34, 36, 38, 42, 47, 59, 74, 85, 87–90, 96, 99–100
efficiency, 12, 42, 47, 59, 70, 85, 87, 89–90, 96, 99–100
employees, 75–78
  new, 76–77
evaluation, 33, 58, 61, 63–66, 68–70, 73–74
  plan, 111
excellence, 2, 5, 10–12, 36, 106, 110
executive director, 8, 23–25, 27–31, 33–35, 39–41, 55, 62–63, 72, 76, 111
executive leadership, 26–27, 34–35, 37, 48, 68
expenses, 29, 55, 62, 66–67, 94–95, 97, 100

F

finances, 15, 18, 29–31, 40, 43, 45, 97–98, 105, 109
financial reports, 29, 96, 98, 101
fiscal agent, 18, 103–4
funders, 43, 53–55, 74, 88–89, 96

funding, 22, 39–40, 95, 97, 100, 111
fundraising, 4, 32, 67, 81, 85, 90

G

gifts, 46, 57, 59, 84
goals, organizational, 2, 20, 22, 32, 34, 42–48, 68, 78, 85, 101
Gold Cup, 9–11, 21, 36, 48, 59, 69, 78, 90, 101
governance, 12, 27, 32, 35, 37–38, 68, 110
  effective, 28, 33
Green-Go, 33

H

honesty, 7–8, 12
human resources, 2–3, 68, 71, 73–74, 77, 79

I

improvement, 4–5, 8–12, 35–36, 59, 68–69, 76, 85–86, 90–91, 99, 106, 110
  organizational, 104, 112
innovations, 25, 49, 85, 87, 89, 91, 100
input, 36, 46–47, 57–59, 100
Internal Revenue Service (IRS), 18, 94
intuition, 62–65, 70

J

job, 4, 25, 40, 48, 54, 62–64, 73–74, 76, 79, 111
  descriptions, 20–21, 32–33, 47–48

K

key leaders, 28, 31–32, 34, 36, 45, 47, 74, 78
key processes, 81, 86–87, 90–91, 106, 110

L

leaders, 8, 11–12, 26–28, 33, 35, 37–38, 48, 53, 57, 77–78, 91, 97, 101, 104, 110, 112
  executive, 31, 36–37, 58

managerial, 37-38
organizational, 20, 44, 98, 100
leadership, 3, 5, 7-8, 22-23, 25-28, 30, 32-33, 35-38, 48, 57, 63, 68-69, 73-74, 86, 90-91, 104-7, 110-11
  components, 28, 38
  effective, 70, 97
  levels, 36
  managerial, 26-27
  organizational, 26-27, 68, 78
  team, 12, 35
  types, 25, 27
legal requirements, 9, 18, 29-31, 44, 56, 66, 74, 88, 98

M

management, 22, 25, 28-29, 47, 63-64, 67-70, 89, 99-101, 104, 106
  practices, 67, 73, 103, 105
measurement, 2, 39, 46-49, 61, 63-70, 87, 90-91, 101, 110-11
  organizational, 100-101
  program effectiveness, 99
  programmatic, 100
meetings, 10, 23-25, 31-33, 35, 40, 62, 67, 72, 81, 95, 104
members, 8, 13, 19, 27, 29-34, 36-37, 40, 43, 47, 53, 55, 57, 75, 77, 94, 98, 106
membership, 21, 53, 83, 94, 104
Minnesota Council of Nonprofits (MCN), 55, 104, 107
mission, 20, 101
  mission statement, 15-16, 19-20, 22, 28, 32, 44-46
  mission/vision/values, 17

N

National Baldrige Quality Program's Criteria for Performance Excellence, 107

nonprofit leaders, 3, 5, 11, 15, 54-55, 70, 104-5
nonprofit organizations, 5, 7-8, 10-11, 14, 16-20, 22, 26-28, 30, 33, 37-38, 43-44, 53-55, 57-58, 61, 65, 67, 71, 74, 76-77, 84-85, 88-89, 94, 96-97, 100-101, 103-7, 109-10, 112
  effectiveness, 26
  excellence, 14, 103-4, 107
  function, 7
  helping, 105
  multifaceted human services, 103
  unique role, 21
nonprofit sector, 5, 14-15, 36, 54, 74
nonprofit tax status, 9, 18

O

objectives, 44, 46-48, 67, 78
operational plans, 46, 48, 77
organization
  accomplishments, 48
  activities, 66
  capacity, 11, 28-29, 34, 36, 43, 47, 78, 109
  goals, 47
  healthy, 11, 97, 109, 111-12
  mission, 15, 21-22, 27, 45, 47, 71
  structure, 28, 110
  values, 17, 22, 31
  vision, 45
  watchdog, 10, 31
outcomes, 8, 10-11, 19, 54, 65, 67, 69, 85, 89-91, 93, 95-96, 98-100, 109-10
outputs, 65, 67, 90, 95, 98, 100, 104

P

patrons, 7, 37, 54-55, 58-59, 86
performance, 2, 11, 35, 37, 48-49, 63-64, 73-74, 76, 85-86, 91, 97, 99, 101, 110-11
  organizational, 68
performance evaluations, 20, 22, 48
performance excellence, 38, 103, 106-7

Performance Excellence Network (PEN), 97, 106
personnel policies, 76
plan
  bad, 112
  long-range, 42
planning, 2, 22, 25, 39, 42-49, 62, 78, 97, 101, 110, 112
  long-range, 45
  operational, 39, 49
  strategic, 43-44, 49
planning process, 46-48
  long-range, 46
  solid, 49
  strategic, 48
policies, 9, 11, 27-28, 30, 32, 35-36, 51, 56, 73-76, 78, 98, 103-4
  best, 11-12
  established, 31, 34
practices, best, 7-8, 88, 101, 103
Principles, 16, 103-4
Principles and Practices of Nonprofit Excellence, 104, 107
processes, 2-5, 8-9, 11-12, 16-18, 21, 28-29, 33, 36-37, 40-41, 43-44, 46, 48, 55-59, 64-66, 68-69, 73-75, 79, 84-91, 100, 103, 105, 110-11
  effective and efficient, 57-58, 88, 90
  measurement, 46, 85
  nonprofit, 88
  service, 90
process improvement, 12, 81, 86-87, 106
products, 19, 49, 51, 53-55, 58-59, 65, 76, 85, 87-88, 90-91, 98, 100-101
program, 2, 8, 14, 18-20, 23-25, 27-28, 40-41, 47, 52, 54, 57-59, 61-69, 73, 77, 85-91, 93, 95-97, 99-101, 106, 109-10
  cost containment, 25
  design, 85, 89, 91
  director, 23-24, 41, 61-62
  evaluation, 61, 70
  management, 68

participants, 2, 7, 43, 54-55, 59, 61, 63, 87, 95, 99
process of delivery, 85, 88-89
program director responsibilities, 62
services, 58
staff, 27-28, 41, 73

Q

quality management, total, 103, 106

R

Red-Stop, 9-10, 18, 29, 44, 56, 66, 74, 88, 98
resources, 5, 15, 31, 43, 46-47, 64-65, 69, 74, 87, 89-90, 96, 99, 105, 111
revenues, 27, 29, 47, 55, 62, 66-67, 90, 94-95, 99, 110

S

sector, social, 4, 13-15, 45, 101
services, 2, 11, 18-19, 27-29, 33, 40-41, 47, 49, 52-59, 71, 76-77, 85-87, 89-91, 93, 97-101, 109
society, 9, 11, 14, 17, 22, 54
staff, 2, 4, 11, 16-17, 20-22, 24, 27-28, 31-32, 35-37, 40-43, 46-48, 51-53, 56, 58, 62-63, 66, 69, 71-79, 82-86, 89-91, 95, 97-101, 104, 111
  leadership, 78
  morale, 77
  satisfaction, 69, 78
stakeholders, 8, 16-17, 21-22, 29, 32, 35-37, 42, 45-46, 48, 51, 54-59, 61, 65-66, 74, 77-78, 87, 89, 91, 96-97, 99, 110, 112
  complaints, 57-58
  current, 59
  data, 31, 57-58, 66
  groups, 43, 58-59
  important, 48
  key, 43, 48
  satisfaction, 52, 56

standards, 10, 33, 67, 78, 91, 101, 105-6
strategic goals, 47, 49, 95, 99
  attainment of, 48
strategic plan, 25, 43-44, 46-48, 112
strategy, 27-28, 47, 110
  potential organizational, 44
subprocesses, 90-91
success, organizational, 37
succession, 73-74, 77
  plans, 36, 78

T

taxes, 98, 101
  filings, 29
total quality management (TQM), 103, 106
transparency, organizational, 30, 35, 45, 57
treasurer, 23, 29, 40, 42, 94

U

United Way (UW), 39-40

V

values, 8-9, 13-17, 19-22, 25-27, 32, 34, 45, 52, 55, 57, 59, 77-79, 99, 111
vision, 13, 15-17, 19-22, 25-27, 32, 34, 37, 44-46, 49, 54, 79, 110
volunteers, 2, 4, 8, 14-16, 19-22, 27-28, 32, 36, 42, 46-48, 51-52, 55-56, 58, 62, 66, 68-69, 71-79, 86, 90, 100-101
  base, 19
  board, 27
  direct service, 28
  engagement, 73
  morale, 76
  new, 51
  regular, 76
  retention, 97

W

workforce, 14, 73-74
work processes, 91

Y

Yellow-Caution, 10, 19, 31, 45, 56, 66-67, 75, 88, 98

If you enjoyed this book, you'll want to pick up the other books in the CharityChannel Press **In the Trenches™** series.

CharityChannel.com/bookstore

CharityChannel PRESS

In addition, there are dozens of titles currently moving to publication.
So be sure to check the CharityChannel.com bookstore.

CharityChannel.com/bookstore

CharityChannel PRESS

And now introducing **For the GENIUS® Press**, an imprint that produces books on just about any topic that people want to learn. You don't have to be a genius to read a **GENIUS** book, but you'll sure be smarter once you do!

Fundraising
Second Edition

for the GENIUS™

A complete course in nonprofit fundraising

Linda Lysakowski

FOR THE GENIUS IN ALL OF US™

ForTheGENIUS.com/bookstore

for the GENIUS PRESS

Caregiving

for the GENIUS™

Understand the Journey from the Inside Out

Jane W. Barton

FOR THE GENIUS IN ALL OF US™

ForTheGENIUS.com/bookstore

for the GENIUS PRESS

Obamacare for the GENIUS

The Affordable Care Act and YOU!

Stacie Harting Marsh

FOR THE GENIUS IN ALL OF US

ForTheGENIUS.com/bookstore

for the GENIUS
PRESS